REPIECING *the* PAST

Patterns for 12 Quilts from the Collection of
SARA RHODES DILLOW

Credits

Technical Editor .... Ursula Reikes
Managing Editor .... Greg Sharp
Design Director .... Judy Petry
Text Designer .... Cheryl Stevenson
Cover Designer .... Joanne Lauterjung
Production Assistant .... Claudia L'Heureux
Illustrator .... Brian Metz
Illustration Assistant .... Lisa McKenney
Copy Editor .... Tina Cook
Proofreaders .... Leslie Phillips
Melissa Riesland
Photographer .... Brent Kane
Photography Assistant .... Richard Lipshay

Repiecing the Past
Patterns for 12 Quilts from the Collection of Sara Rhodes Dillow
© 1995 by Sara Rhodes Dillow
That Patchwork Place, Inc., PO Box 118
Bothell, WA 98041-0118 USA

Printed in the United States of America
00 99 98 97 96 95   6 5 4 3 2 1

Library of Congress Cataloging-in-Publication Data

Dillow, Sara Rhodes,
   Repiecing the past : patterns for 12 quilts from the collection of Sara Rhodes Dillow.
      p.   cm.
   Includes bibliographical references.
   ISBN 1-56477-129-6
   1. Patchwork—Patterns. 2. Patchwork quilts. I. Title.
TT835.D56   1995
746.46—dc20   95-38724
                                                    CIP

Mission Statement

We are dedicated to providing quality products that encourage creativity and promote self-esteem in our customers and our employees.

We strive to make a difference in the lives we touch.

That Patchwork Place is an employee-owned, financially secure company.

Dedication

To my great-great grandmother, Rebecca Wilson, and my great-grandmother, Isabelle Irene Wilson Rhodes.

To all the quiltmakers of yesteryear for stitching the fabric of their lives—our heritage.

Acknowledgments

My deepest appreciation to:

Jean Gausman, for making a quilt for this book and always answering just one more, "What do you think?" question.

Judy McClure, Kathy Murphy, and June Vogltance, for piecing and quilting quilts for this book.

Mary Burmester, my "right hand needle," for her assistance whenever I needed help.

The Basket Cases, for creating a true friendship quilt.

Margrethe Ahlschwede, Judy Lane, and Lois Wilson, for their lovely appliqué blocks and special friendship.

Alberta Martens, for the beautifully designed labels for every quilt.

Anna Goeken, Martha Lane, Alberta Nichols, and Nancy Wylie, for their hand quilting.

Nancy J. Martin, for suggesting the idea for this book.

My husband and collecting partner, Byron. My love and thanks for his never-ending patience and toleration of yet another project.

The lights of our lives, our children and their spouses: Dave and Gwen, Jeff and Beth, Ann and Tim. My love and appreciation for their encouragement and support.

Contents

Preface 6

Introduction 6

Collecting Quilts 6

Caring for Quilts 7

Cleaning Quilts 8

Keeping Records 9

Quilt Patterns 9

    Fascinating Colors 10

    Rolling Stones Gather Friends 17

    Rebecca's Legacy 21

    For Megan 25

    Hexagonal Magic 28

    Blooms! Blooms! Blooms! 32

    Fireside Fantasy 40

    The Dishes Are Done 43

    Star Garden 47

    Bears in the Woods 57

    Drifting Leaves 63

    Amber Waves of Grain 67

Quiltmaking Basics 72

Finishing Techniques 79

Resources & Bibliography 84

Templates 85

About the Author 87

Galleries 13, 33, 53

Preface

In 1982 Nancy J. Martin spent an afternoon at my home during a visit to Lincoln, Nebraska, to attend the annual seminar of The American Quilt Study Group. We had a wonderful time sharing stories about our passion for quilts and the quiltmaking process. It was during her visit that Nancy suggested the idea for this book—taking a pattern from an antique quilt and adapting it for today's quilters. The concept appealed to me because it combined two of my passions: learning from history and making quilts.

Our quilting heritage traveled in covered wagons and in the sewing boxes of quiltmakers as the settlers of our country moved west. Quiltmakers of the past made quilts by hand, using limited resources. Today's quiltmakers use time-saving techniques, higher quality fabrics, and have more tools at their disposal. But one thing remains constant: Quiltmakers love to make quilts!

Antique quilts offer inspiration, insight, and a never-ending array of information. These fragile treasures are diaries of fabrics, construction techniques, patterns, regional influences, and trends. It is a privilege to learn from the work of early quiltmakers. The work of their hands, the stitches of their lives, have been entrusted to us. A quilt made from a century-old design preserves our quiltmaking heritage and continues the chain of stitches uniting all quilters.

Introduction

Repiecing the Past includes twelve quilt patterns, which I adapted from quilts in my collection. For your inspiration, the antique quilts are shown with their modern adaptations in the gallery. This gives you an opportunity to compare the fabrics and colors in the two quilts. The original quilts were made between 1859 and 1924.

Some of the patterns in this book have survived beautifully over the years, passed down from one generation to the next through exchanges with neighbors, peddlers, quilting bees, families, and friends. Other patterns were not so fortunate. I researched the history of each pattern as best I could and included this information with each quilt. Unfortunately, some of the quilts have no documented history. For these, I tried to speculate why the quilt may have been made, or how its pattern may have developed.

Complete instructions are provided for making the new quilts, including quick-piecing and rotary-cutting techniques wherever possible. "Quiltmaking Basics" on pages 72–79 includes directions for these modern-day methods, and "Finishing Techniques" on pages 79–83 covers techniques for completing your quilts. Templates are provided for the patterns where necessary.

Quiltmaking is a pleasure. There are no rules of right or wrong. Enjoy the process and the product. Quiltmaking offers satisfaction, pride, growth, and involvement in a wonderful community of people known as quilters. Enjoy!

Collecting Quilts

It began so innocently! A trip to an antique show and then an unexpected flip-flop of the heart when a wonderful quilt came into sight. After a little discussion, my husband and I concluded that it would be okay to buy "just this one quilt." Several years and several quilts later, we realized our love affair with quilts had resulted in a collection that we appreciate emotionally as well as artistically. It has been gratifying to learn that our quilts are of interest to others.

Since that innocent beginning, we have grown in our knowledge of collecting and in our understanding of what it means to have a collection. And we are still learning.

People collect quilts for a number of reasons. Some look for quilts with intriguing histories; other collectors buy quilts simply because they enjoy them.

Other reasons people collect quilts include:

★ A fondness for a particular type of quilt
★ A fascination with the fabrics in a particular quilt
★ A feeling of connection with the past
★ A desire to learn about fabrics and quiltmaking techniques

Every quilt collector approaches collecting in a personal way. My husband Byron and I collect together, which doubles the "checkpoints" when we consider purchasing a quilt. First, we must be attracted to the quilt; let's call that the "flip-flop" test. Other variables we consider before making the purchase decision include:

★ The condition of the quilt in relation to its rarity
★ The documentation available with the quilt
★ The cost of the quilt in relation to the market
★ The special qualities of the quilt
★ The seriousness of the "flip-flop" factor

We both have to agree before we purchase a quilt for the collection.

Each collection has its own flavor and a sometimes imperceptible quality that reflects the personality of the collector. For me, that is the charm of collecting. It is individual, unique, and satisfying. Some collectors set goals and strive to assemble a collection that meets those goals. These collections might reflect:

★ Quilts from a specific geographic area
★ Quilts from a specific time period
★ Quilts that reflect the chronology of American quiltmaking
★ Quilts featuring a particular construction technique; for example, appliqué
★ Quilts with specific historical significance

The pleasures of a collection are personal and long lasting. An antique quilt collection, no matter how small or large, offers great interest and information. The quilts connect us with the history of our craft and with the amazing quiltmakers of earlier years. Without electricity for sewing machines or illumination, without rotary cutters, without computers and their exciting new quilt programs, and without sophisticated measuring devices, early textile artists created an incredible body of work.

It is probably obvious that I am sentimental about quilts and their makers. Well, yes, I am, and I am proud of it. Quilts have enriched and warmed my life—collectively!

Caring for Quilts

Quilts and textiles are delicate, fragile artifacts. Collectors are obligated to provide the best care possible to preserve their treasures. In addition to the physical care of quilts, a collector needs to keep a record of the quilt, including documentation, acquisition information, and details on its condition.

The care of quilts and textiles is a young science. Quilts are extremely sensitive to chemicals, dust, dirt, moisture, oils, light, smoke, perfumes, cosmetics, and excessive laundering. Methods for the care of antique quilts are continually improving. The quilt-care suggestions included here apply to both new quilts and antique quilts.

The first step in the care of any quilt is to document it with a photograph. Refer to it periodically to determine if any fading or other changes are taking place. The photograph acts as a standard, and when compared to the quilt, may show subtle changes that the casual eye would not observe.

Quilt Care Tips

* Avoid exposure to direct sunlight.
* Use ultraviolet-light filters on windows, and filter or protect quilts from fluorescent light when on display.
* Keep your storage area's temperature and humidity comfortable.
* Handle quilts as little as possible, and only with very clean hands or while wearing clean gloves.
* Keep your storage area free from insects.
* If you fold a quilt, refold it every few months to keep permanent creases from forming, or wad up acid-free tissue and place it in the quilt folds.

Quilt Display Tips

* A fabric casing or sleeve stitched to the top edge of the quilt back is ideal for hanging a quilt; see directions for sleeve construction on page 83.
* Distribute the weight of the quilt along the entire hanging edge.
* Give quilts that are hung for display a rest periodically.
* Do not display quilts in a traffic area where they may be handled or rubbed.

Cleaning Quilts

Each quilt is unique and most likely irreplaceable. When cleaning quilts, it is better to err on the side of caution than to risk ruining one. When in doubt about cleaning a quilt, do not attempt it. Never clean a quilt at a commercial dry cleaner. The chemicals and agitation used in the cleaning process are very harmful to quilts.

Wash quilts only as a last resort. Evaluate the condition of each quilt carefully before deciding to wash it. Always test for colorfastness. Gently rub one of the fabrics with a moistened cotton swab. If the color rubs off on the swab, then the dye will run in washing. Test every fabric in the same manner. If the dyes appear to be coming off, do not attempt to wash the quilt. Consider vacuuming the quilt instead, as instructed below.

If you decide to wash a quilt, use a mild soap such as Orvus® or Ensure. Prepare a solution of soap and warm water in a sink or bathtub; do not wash your quilts in a washing machine. Gently move the quilt around in the water. Let the water drain; then rinse with cool water. Rinse at least three times to be sure that the soap is removed from the fabric.

Squeeze the quilt gently to remove excess water; never wring or twist. Place the quilt flat on a large towel or sheet to dry.

A safe alternative to washing a quilt is to vacuum it. This method places the least amount of stress on fragile fabrics. Place a fiberglass screen on top of the quilt and gently hand-vacuum with the machine on low power. This will not remove stains embedded in the fibers, but it will remove dust and dirt that may have accumulated over the years.

DO NOT:

* Store quilts in plastic bags; they need to breathe.
* Smoke near quilts or textiles.
* Hang quilts with tacks, nails, or metal clips.
* Store quilts in cedar chests, closets, or directly on wood. Place a layer of muslin or cotton flannel between the quilt and the wood.
* Refold quilts on the same lines. Rotate your folding methods to avoid creases.

Keeping Records

Keep a written record of your quilt collection. Do this for new quilts as well as for antique quilts. Photograph the quilt when it comes into your possession. Keep notes on the origin of the quilt, any history or special information that is associated with the quilt, the purchase price (or fabric cost), where and from whom it was purchased, its physical condition, and any other information that is unique to that quilt. If photographs of the maker are available, be sure to protect and include them with your records.

We attach an archival tag to each quilt in our collection with a string and a small brass safety pin. The tag lists the name of the quilt and its number in the collection. You can sew a label to the quilt back for identification; however, antique quilts are fragile, and using a needle on a brittle fabric may cause additional deterioration or stress.

Quilt Patterns

Study the original quilts and their modern-day adaptations in the galleries. Read through "Quiltmaking Basics" on pages 72–79 before beginning the quilts in this book. Then use your needle and thread to repiece the past.

Name of Quilt:

Collection Number:

Date of Purchase:

Purchase Price:

Dealer Name and Address:

Measurements of Quilt: (width x length)

Condition of Quilt:

Quiltmaker's Name:

Additional Information:

Dating Information:

    Fabric (color, print):

    Quilting (pattern, method):

    Pattern (name, origin):

Notes:

Photograph of Quilt and/or Quiltmaker:

Antique Quilt

Crossed Laurel Leaves

Quilt Size: 86" x 104"

Color photo on page 13

Origin: Pennsylvania, 1859

Construction: This quilt is dated 1859 in the quilting stitches, along with the initials WLS. It was hand appliquéd and hand quilted, and has an applied binding.

The Crossed Laurel Leaves pattern was a popular design, as evidenced by its use in many appliqué quilts in the mid—eighteen hundreds. The album quilts made in the Baltimore, Maryland, area in the 1850s often included a Crossed Laurel Leaves block. Laurel foliage was used by the ancient Greeks to crown victors in the Pythian games. Upon completion of this quilt, we would hope the quiltmaker felt like a victor. She created a distinctive and visually exciting quilt.

New Quilt

Fascinating Colors

Quilt Size: 53½" x 53½"

Finished Block Size: 14"

Materials: 44"-wide fabric

⅜ yd. gold for leaves and flowers
1⅝ yds. red for leaves, inner border, and binding
1⅝ yds. green for leaves, stems, and outer border
2⅜ yds. navy blue for background
3¼ yds. for backing

Cutting

Measurements include ¼"-wide seam allowances. Cut all strips from the lengthwise grain of the fabric. Cut strips before cutting template pieces. Use the templates on page 85.

From gold fabric, cut:
   36 of Template 1
   12 of Template 2

From red fabric, cut:
   4 strips, each 2" x 48", for inner border
   5 strips, each 2¼" x 54", for binding
   108 of Template 1

From green fabric, cut:
   4 strips, each 4½" x 55", for outer border
   18 strips, each ¾" x 14", for stems
   144 of Template 1

From navy blue fabric, cut:
   9 squares, each 16" x 16", for background squares. The squares are oversized. They will be trimmed after the appliqué has been completed.

(Instructions continued on page 12)

Quilt Plan

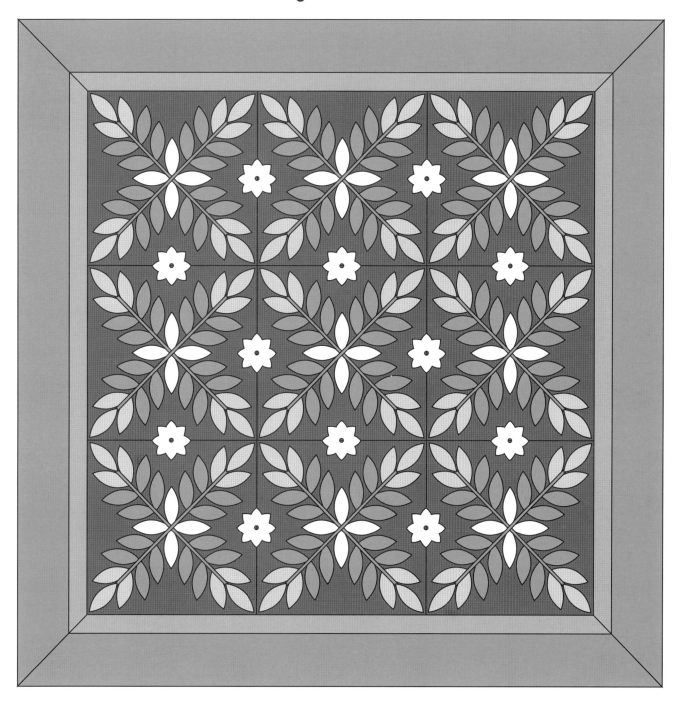

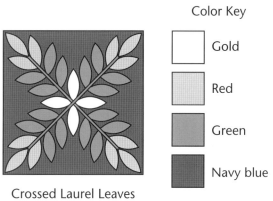

Crossed Laurel Leaves

Color Key

Gold

Red

Green

Navy blue

Appliquéing the Blocks

1. Fold a 16" square of tracing paper twice diagonally. Unfold the paper and align the diagonal lines on the tracing paper with the lines of the quarter-pattern provided on the pullout. Trace the leaves and the stem placement on the diagonal line. Repeat with the other 3 diagonal lines to make a full-size pattern of the Crossed Laurel Leaves appliqué block.

2. Fold a navy blue background square in half diagonally and press. Open, fold on the other diagonal, and press.

3. Lay the creased navy blue square on the full-size pattern. Match the diagonal creases in the fabric with the diagonal lines on your traced pattern. Use a contrasting-color pencil to trace the complete design onto the navy blue square. Trace ⅛" inside the pattern lines to ensure that the appliqué will cover the traced lines. Use a light box to help you see the pattern through dark fabric.

4. Appliqué 2 gold, 4 green, and 2 red leaves on each diagonal line. Do not appliqué the red leaf at the end of the stem until after you have appliquéd the stem. See "Appliqué Techniques" on pages 75–77.

5. Fold the ¾" x 14" green stems in thirds and press. Baste along the center of the stem to keep the folds in place.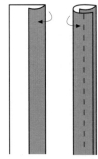

6. Pin the stems on the diagonal lines, just covering the tips of the appliquéd leaves. Appliqué in place.

7. Appliqué a red leaf at each end of the diagonal stems.

8. Use a large square ruler to trim the blocks to 14½" x 14½". Center the design and trim all 4 sides of the block; otherwise your design will be lopsided.

Assembling and Finishing the Quilt

1. Sew the appliquéd blocks together in 3 rows of 3 blocks each. Press the seams in opposite directions from row to row. Join the rows.

2. Appliqué the gold flowers in the spaces between blocks; refer to the quilt plan on page 11. Use the reverse-appliqué technique to make the flower centers. Draw a small circle on the center of a flower. Carefully cut away the inside of the circle, ⅛" inside the drawn line. Clip the edges to the drawn line. Roll under the seam allowance and appliqué around the circle.

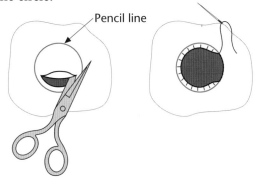

Pencil line

3. Sew each 2"-wide inner-border strip to a 4½"-wide outer-border strip. Treat the resulting unit as a single border strip. Measure, cut, and sew the border strips to the quilt top, referring to "Borders with Mitered Corners" on pages 78–79.

4. Refer to "Finishing Techniques" on pages 79–83. Layer quilt top with batting and backing; baste. Quilt as desired or follow the quilting suggestion. Bind the edges of the quilt.

5. Label your quilt.

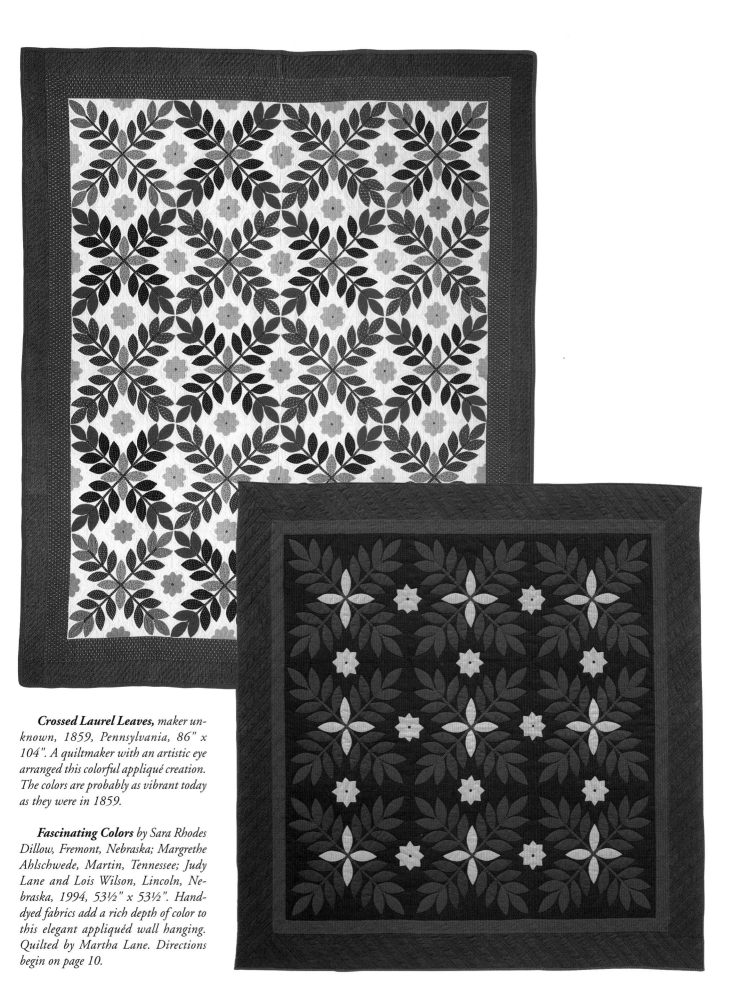

Crossed Laurel Leaves, *maker unknown, 1859, Pennsylvania, 86" x 104". A quiltmaker with an artistic eye arranged this colorful appliqué creation. The colors are probably as vibrant today as they were in 1859.*

Fascinating Colors *by Sara Rhodes Dillow, Fremont, Nebraska; Margrethe Ahlschwede, Martin, Tennessee; Judy Lane and Lois Wilson, Lincoln, Nebraska, 1994, 53½" x 53½". Hand-dyed fabrics add a rich depth of color to this elegant appliquéd wall hanging. Quilted by Martha Lane. Directions begin on page 10.*

Princess Feather by Rebecca Wilson and Isabella Irene Wilson Rhodes, 1865, Knox County, Ohio, 84" x 84". This four-block quilt is a beautiful example of the red-and-green appliqué quilts created in the mid–eighteen hundreds.

Rebecca's Legacy by Sara Rhodes Dillow, 1994, Fremont, Nebraska, 87½" x 87½". Appliquéing the Princess Feather pattern that my ancestors made more than one hundred years ago was a sentimental journey. A bond seemed to exist, or perhaps it was a common thread, connecting the old and new quilts. Directions begin on page 21.

Oak Leaf and Swag, *maker unknown, ca. 1860–70, 26½" x 33½". Purchased in Douglas County, Nebraska. This pink-and-green appliqué cradle quilt probably came west with settlers.*

For Megan *by Sara Rhodes Dillow, 1994, Fremont, Nebraska, 26½" x 35". While working on this cradle-quilt replica, I told my friends that it was for my first grandchild, whenever that child would arrive. Before the quilt was completed, Dave and Gwen announced they were expecting my first grandchild. Megan Leigh Dillow was born on November 27, 1994, making this quilt "For Megan." Quilted by Anna Goeken. Collection of Megan Dillow. Directions begin on page 25.*

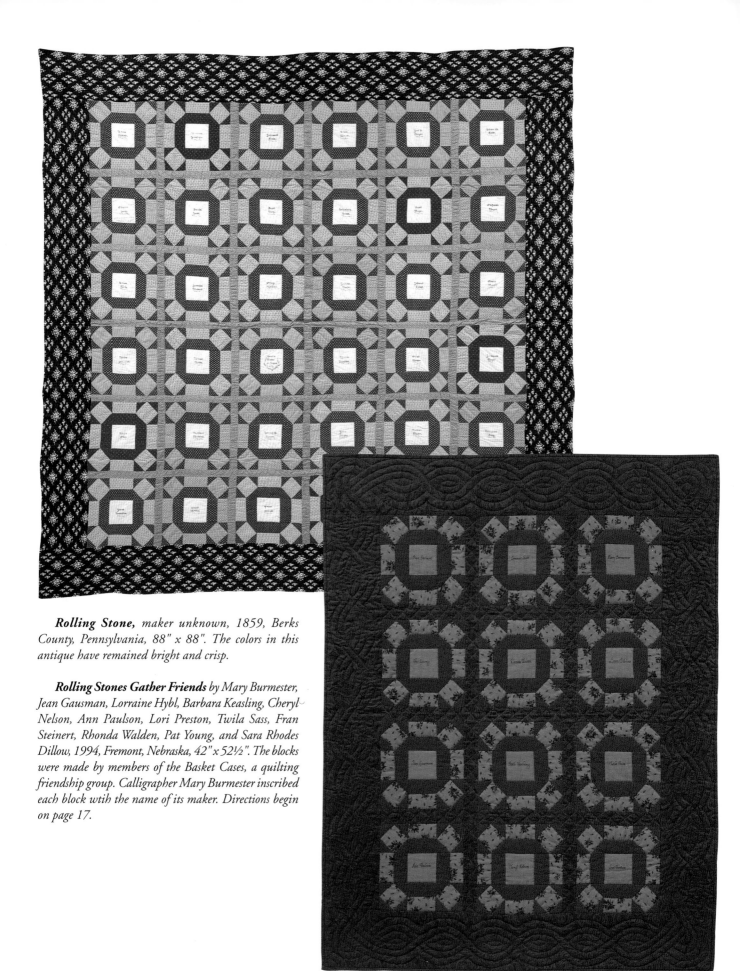

Rolling Stone, *maker unknown, 1859, Berks County, Pennsylvania, 88" x 88". The colors in this antique have remained bright and crisp.*

Rolling Stones Gather Friends *by Mary Burmester, Jean Gausman, Lorraine Hybl, Barbara Keasling, Cheryl Nelson, Ann Paulson, Lori Preston, Twila Sass, Fran Steinert, Rhonda Walden, Pat Young, and Sara Rhodes Dillow, 1994, Fremont, Nebraska, 42" x 52½". The blocks were made by members of the Basket Cases, a quilting friendship group. Calligrapher Mary Burmester inscribed each block wtih the name of its maker. Directions begin on page 17.*

Antique Quilt

Rolling Stone

Quilt Size: 88" x 88"
Color photo on page 16

Origin: Berks County,
Pennsylvania, 1859

Construction: The quilt was hand pieced and hand quilted. White thread was used to quilt the blocks and tan thread was used to quilt the border. The navy blue floral used for the border was turned under to finish the quilt edges. A delightful brown diamond print was used for the backing.

This design may have been named by an industrious nineteenth-century quiltmaker inspired by the adage "A rolling stone gathers no moss." This block is sometimes called Squirrel in a Cage or Broken Wheel.

The names on the thirty-six blocks were written in ink in elaborate German script, known as "Fraktur." The scribing was probably done by an itinerant Fraktur writer.

One of the thirty-six ink-inscribed blocks done in Fraktur lettering, which reads "Sophia Moser her rug [quilt], 1859."

New Quilt

Rolling Stones Gather Friends

Quilt Size: 42" x 52¹⁄₂"
Finished Block Size: 9"

This quilt was made by the Basket Cases quilting friendship group. Mary Burmester, a calligrapher, lettered the quilters' names on their blocks.

Materials: 44"-wide fabric

¼ yd. olive for center squares
⅝ yd. floral print for corner squares and rectangles
¾ yd. red for small triangles and rectangles
1⅜ yds. khaki for sashing, border, and binding
3¼ yds. for backing

Cutting

Measurements include ¼"-wide seam allowances. Cut all strips across the width of the fabric (crosswise grain).

(Cutting instructions continued on page 19)

Quilt Plan

Color Key

	Olive
	Floral print
	Red
	Khaki

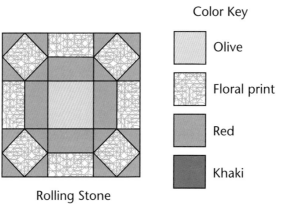

Rolling Stone

From olive fabric, cut:
    1 strip, 3½" x 42"; crosscut into 12 squares, each 3½" x 3½"

From floral print, cut:
    3 strips, each 2⅝" x 42"; crosscut into 48 squares, each 2⅝" x 2⅝"
    4 strips, each 2" x 42"

From red fabric, cut:
    6 strips, each 2⅜" x 42"; crosscut into 96 squares, each 2⅜" x 2⅜". Cut the squares once diagonally to yield 192 half-square triangles.
    4 strips, each 2" x 42"

From khaki fabric, cut:
    2 strips, each 2" wide; crosscut into 8 strips, each 2" x 9½", for horizontal sashing
    2 strips, each 2" x 41", for vertical sashing
    4 strips, each 6¼" x 42", for borders
    5 strips, each 2¼" x 42", for binding

Assembling the Blocks

I. Sew 2 red triangles to opposite sides of a 2⅝" floral square; then sew 2 more red triangles to the remaining sides to make a corner square. Press seams toward triangles.

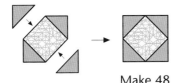

Make 48

2. Sew a 2"-wide floral strip to a 2"-wide red strip to make a strip unit. Cut the strip units into a total of 48 segments, each 3½" wide.

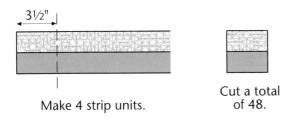

Make 4 strip units.

Cut a total of 48.

3. Sew the center square, rectangle segments, and corner squares together in horizontal rows. Press the seams toward the rectangle segments.

Join the rows to complete the block.

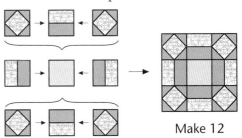

Make 12

Assembling and Finishing the Quilt

I. Sew 4 blocks and 3 khaki horizontal sashing strips together to make a vertical row of blocks. Make 3 rows.

2. Sew the khaki vertical sashing strips between the rows of blocks. Carefully match the seam lines of the blocks across the sashing strips.

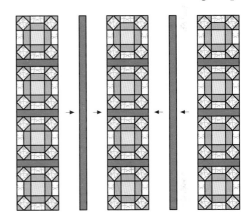

3. Measure, cut, and sew the 6¼"-wide border strips to the quilt top, referring to "Straight-Cut Borders" on pages 77–78.

4. Refer to "Finishing Techniques" on pages 79–83. Layer the quilt top with batting and backing; baste. Quilt as desired or follow the quilting suggestion. Bind the edges of the quilt.

5. Label your quilt.

Antique Quilt

Princess Feather

Quilt Size: 84" x 84"
Color photo on page 14

Origin: Knox County,
Ohio, 1865

Construction: This quilt was hand appliquéd and hand quilted. The binding is applied.

Princess Feather Quilt
1865
Made and quilted by Mrs.
Rebecca Wilson and daughter Belle
(later Mrs. J. L. Rhodes) in Knox Co. Ohio.

While working on quilt word was
received of assination of President
Lincoln

"Princess Feather" was made by Rebecca Wilson (1829—99) and Isabella Irene Wilson Rhodes (1850—1929). It was taken to Beatrice, Gage County, Nebraska, in the late 1870s.

This mother and daughter, my great-great grandmother and great-grandmother, were working on this quilt when they received word of the assassination of President Lincoln. This was documented by my great-aunt, Clara Rhodes, Isabella Irene's daughter. Aunt Clara willed this quilt to me with a note pinned to the quilt (see photo below left).

Because of the quality of work in this quilt, and because it was made after the Civil War had just ended, I almost feel as though it was a quilt of celebration. "Princess Feather" is the only known surviving quilt made by these two women. As quiltmakers and skilled needleworkers, one assumes that Rebecca and "Belle" Irene were involved with other Knox County, Ohio, women in making quilts as bedding for soldiers, or were using their needles to provide funds for the war effort.

Princess Feather quilts have traditionally been appliquéd in red

Rebecca and Alexander Wilson (above left) photographed in the late 1870s after they had settled in Gage County, Nebraska. Rebecca made the Princess Feather quilt with her daughter, Isabella Irene Wilson Rhodes, in Knox County, Ohio, in 1865.

Isabella Irene Wilson Rhodes and her husband, John L. Rhodes (above right), around 1880.

and green. Green dyes were not readily available until 1875, so the green fabric in the antique appliqué is overdyed. Plain fabric was colored by first dyeing the fabric blue and then overdyeing with yellow to make green. This method was used by both professional and home dyers in the mid-eighteen hundreds. Were Rebecca and "Belle" Irene home dyers? We can only speculate!

The design source for the Princess Feather pattern is attributed to the plumes in the Prince of Wales's hat. Can you picture the graceful movement as the breezes touched the plumage of his hat? In my mind, the feathers had to be white. Was the feather from a great egret's plumage? It's easy to imagine "Prince's" Feather gradually becoming "Princess" Feather. Other names for this design are Star and Plumes and Ben Hur's Chariot Wheel.

More recently, Ricky Clark suggests in her book "Quilted Gardens, Floral Quilts of the Nineteenth Century," that the inspiration for the Prince's Feather might have been a plant known as "Amaranthus hypochondriacus," which was grown in early settlers' gardens. Irene Hardy recalls in her book, "The Making of a Schoolmistress, 1913," that this plant was sometimes called "kiss-me-over-the-fence." An earlier book, "Gray's School and Field Book of Botany," printed in 1876, lists "Amaranthus caudatus" as Princes' Feather. It describes "A. caudatus" as having "leaves ovate, bright green; spikes red, naked, long and slender, in a drooping panicle, the terminal one forming a very long tail."

Rebecca's Legacy

Quilt Size: 87½" x 87½"
Finished Block Size: 34"

My initial plans were to make the "new" quilt in different colors. But sentimentality won! It was a personal journey to re-create this quilt made by relatives I never met. I wondered what thoughts and concerns were stitched into their quilt and what anguish they must have felt at hearing of Lincoln's assassination. As I appliquéd the new Princess Feather quilt, thoughts of my family and concerns of the times were also stitched into its fabric.

Materials: 44"-wide fabric

2 yds. red for small and large plumes
4 yds. green for small and large plumes, stars, vine, and binding
7 yds. tone-on-tone fabric for background and border

Cutting

Measurements include ¼"-wide seam allowances. Cut strips across the width of the fabric (crosswise grain) unless otherwise instructed. Use the templates on the pullout pattern and on page 85.

From red fabric, cut:
8 of Template 1
8 of Template 1 reversed
12 of Template 2

From green fabric, cut:
8 of Template 1
8 of Template 1 reversed
12 of Template 2 reversed
4 of Template 3
9 strips, each 2¼" x 42", for binding
Use the remainder of the fabric to cut ¾"-wide bias strips. You will need approximately 400" of bias for the vine in the outer border.

(Cutting instructions continued on page 23)

Color Key

Red

Green

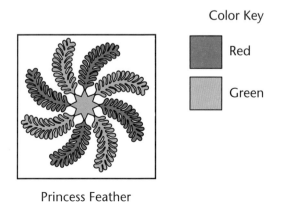

Princess Feather

NOTE: To rough-cut the plumes and stars, trace around the templates on the right side of the fabric. Cut around the entire shape of the plume. Do not cut between the petals of the plume. You will cut these as you appliqué. See "Cut-As-You-Go Appliqué" on page 77.

From tone-on-tone background fabric, cut:
    4 squares, each 38" x 38". These are slightly oversized and will be trimmed after the appliqué has been completed.
    4 strips, each 10" x 94", from the lengthwise grain of the fabric

Appliquéing the Blocks

I. Fold the 38" background squares in half, then in half again to find the center; finger-press. Unfold the square and position Template 3 on the center of the square and lightly mark around the template with a pencil.

2. Position the bottom of a rough-cut large red plume on one of the points of the traced star so that the end will be covered by the star point when the star is appliquéd. Pin in place.

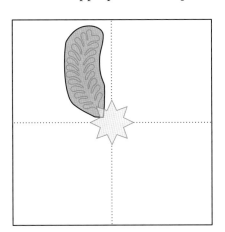

Position 3 more red plumes and 4 green plumes on the star points; alternating the colors of the plumes and making sure that they are all facing the same direction. Make 2 blocks with the plumes facing one direction and 2 blocks with the plumes facing in the opposite direction. Refer to the quilt plan on page 22.

3. Appliqué the plumes in place. Refer to "Cut-As-You-Go Appliqué" on page 77. Use ½"-long sequin pins to hold the fabric while appliquéing.

4. Appliqué a green star in the center of the background square, covering the end of the plumes with a star point.

5. Trim the blocks to 34½" x 34½". Be sure to trim from all 4 sides of the background square; otherwise the design will be lopsided.

Assembling and Finishing the Quilt

I. Sew the blocks together in 2 rows of 2 blocks each. Join the rows.

2. Sew the 10"-wide border strips to the quilt top, referring to "Borders with Mitered Corners" on pages 78–79.

3. Sew the ends of the ¾"-wide bias strips together to make one long, continuous strip. Fold the strip in thirds and press; then baste along the center of the stem.

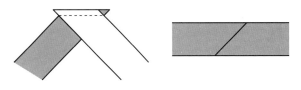

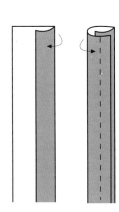

4. Using the Vine Placement Guide on the pullout pattern, trace 2 corner sections, 3 red sections, and 2 green sections onto tracing paper. Tape the paper sections together to make a full-size guide for the border, as shown in the diagram on the pullout pattern. Shorten or lengthen the vine as necessary to fit the border on your quilt. Place each border of the quilt onto the traced pattern and lightly trace the design.

5. Appliqué the small red and green plumes. Appliqué vine, covering the ends of the plumes.
6. Refer to "Finishing Techniques" on pages 79–83. Layer quilt top with batting and backing; baste. Quilt as desired or follow the quilting suggestion below. Bind the edges of the quilt.
7. Label your quilt.

Antique Quilt

Oak Leaf and Swag

Quilt Size: 26½" x 33½"
Color photo on page 15

Origin: Elkhorn, Nebraska,
circa 1860–70

Construction: The pink flowers were applied with a fine buttonhole stitch, while all the other appliqué was done with a blind stitch. The quilting was done in white thread. The same white fabric was used for the back, and a binding was applied to finish the quilt.

Botanical references are frequently found in nineteenth-century literature and diaries. Settlers carried seeds and seedlings across the country, because plants were important for their survival. The quiltmaker may have been projecting a symbol of strength by using the oak leaf on her quilt. This is probably a desirable image for a cradle quilt, in the hope that the baby might grow to be mighty like an oak.

The swag shape is common to the appliqué work of the period. Architectural motifs may have provided an observant quiltmaker with the design.

The fabrics in this quilt have deteriorated over the years. The green swags, flower petals, and oak leaves may have been more vibrant when the unknown quilter's hands worked on this small piece.

It is romantic to think that the same hands that created this quilt rocked a beautiful cradle holding her firstborn, sleeping peacefully, warmed by this quilt. Imagine the light of a candle and a young husband standing nearby, proud of the cradle he made himself.

New Quilt

For Megan

Quilt Size: 26½" x 35"

Materials: 44"-wide fabric

¼ yd. pink for oak leaves, center flowers, and petal flower centers

¼ yd. pink for small flowers, petal flower centers, and ends of bows

⅓ yd. green for leaves and swags

1⅛ yds. tone-on-tone for background
1⅛ yds. for backing
¼ yd. for binding

Cutting

Use the templates on the pullout pattern.

From pink #1 fabric, cut:
2 of Template 1
1 of Template 2
8 of Template 6

(Cutting instructions continued on page 27)

Quilt Plan

Color Key

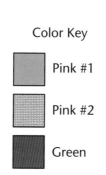

Pink #1

Pink #2

Green

From pink #2 fabric, cut:
    2 of Template 1
    10 of Template 5
    8 of Template 7

From green fabric, cut:
    4 of Template 2
    10 of Template 3
    34 of Template 4
    4 of Template 8

From background fabric, cut:
    1 piece, 27" x 35½"

Appliquéing the Quilt Top

I. Make a paper pattern of one-half of the design. Trace the quarter design on the pullout pattern onto 2 pieces of paper. Tracing paper or tissue paper is preferable because you can see through the design easily from both sides. Turn 1 of the pieces over and trace the design onto the other side. Tape the pieces together, matching the center lines. If you cannot see the design through the paper, place the pattern piece on a light table or window and trace the design on the other side of the paper.

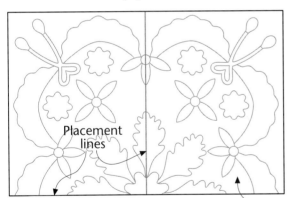

Tape two quarters together
to make half of the design.

Trace from
reverse side.

2. Fold the quilt top in half and then in half again. Press the folds to mark the center horizontal and vertical lines. Place the paper pattern on a light table or tape it to a window. Then place the top half of the quilt top on the pattern. Matching the vertical and horizontal lines, pin or tape the fabric in place. Lightly trace the design onto the quilt top just inside the pattern lines. Turn the paper pattern 180°, placing it under the bottom half of the quilt top (or turn the quilt top around 180°). Match the horizontal and vertical creases with the corresponding placement lines on the pattern. Trace the pattern to complete the design.

3. Appliqué the pieces in numerical order. Refer to "Appliqué Techniques" on pages 75–77.

Finishing the Quilt

I. Refer to "Finishing Techniques" on pages 79–83. Layer the quilt top with batting and backing; baste. Quilt as desired or follow the quilting suggestion. Cut 3 strips, each 2¼" x 42", from fabric for binding and bind the edges of the quilt.

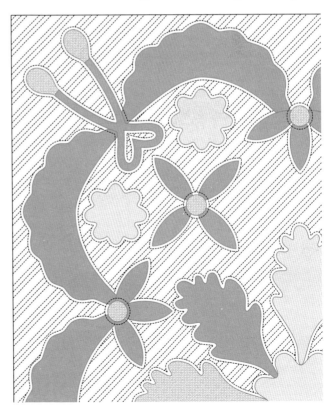

2. Label your quilt.

Antique Quilt

Honeycomb Patch

Quilt Size: 72" x 83½"
Color photo on page 34

Origin: Indiana,
circa 1870–80

Construction: This quilt was hand pieced and hand quilted. The front border was turned to the back to finish the edges.

Nature provides inspiration for quilters, including design shapes. The Honeycomb pattern uses a hexagon, which is a geometric shape used often by quiltmakers, as well as by bees!

Beekeeping was common in the 1880s. It provided honey for settlers' food supplies and crop pollinators for their orchards.

This quilt features hexagons, triangles, and diamonds in dynamic colors. The design is similar to a Grandmother's Flower Garden, but the setting differs slightly with the use of setting diamonds and triangles.

Hexagons are most often pieced by hand using a method known as English paper piecing. The paper hexagons stabilize the fabric as the pieces are whipstitched together. The paper is then removed when the piecing is complete.

New Quilt

Hexagonal Magic

Quilt Size: 40" x 56½"

Materials: 44"-wide fabric

3 yds. of assorted fabrics for blocks and binding
1 yd. black for inner border and diamonds
1½ yds. purple for triangles and border
1⅔ yds. for backing
½ yd. for binding
Freezer paper

Cutting

Measurements include ¼"-wide seam allowances. Cut all strips from the lengthwise grain of the fabric. Use the templates on page 86.

From freezer paper, cut:
264 of Template 1
216 of Template 2
80 of Template 3

NOTE: Do not add seam allowances when cutting freezer-paper templates. Iron the freezer-paper templates to the wrong side of the fabrics listed below. Add ¼"-wide seam allowances all around when cutting fabric.

(Cutting instructions continued on page 30)

Quilt Plan

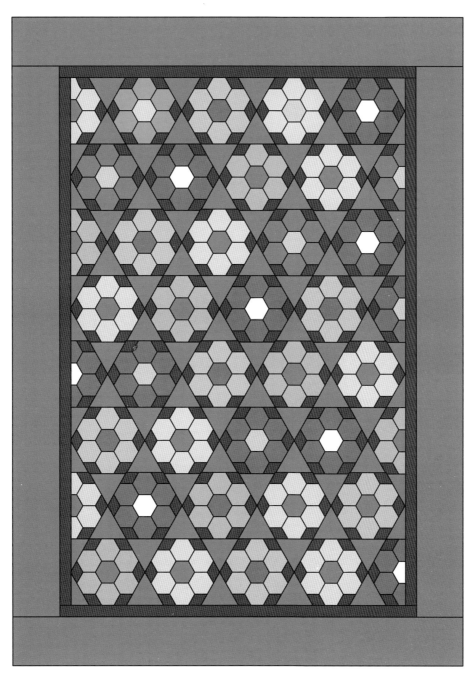

Color Key

Assorted colors

Black

Purple

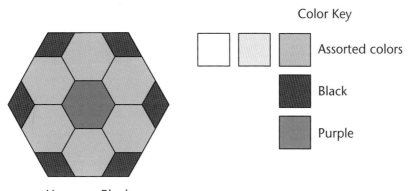

Hexagon Block

From assorted fabrics, cut:
    264 of Template 1

From black fabric, cut:
    2 strips, each 1½" x 48", for inner side border
    2 strips, each 1½" x 32", for inner top and bottom borders
    216 of Template 2

From purple fabric, cut:
    2 strips, each 4½" x 50", for outer side border
    2 strips, each 4½" x 42", for outer top and bottom border
    80 of Template 3

From fabric for binding, cut:
    5 strips, each 2¼" x 42"

Assembling the Blocks

I. Finger-press the seam allowance over the freezer-paper hexagons. With right sides facing and edges aligned, whipstitch a black center hexagon to an outside hexagon cut from the assorted fabrics. Whipstitch a total of 6 hexagons around a center hexagon to make a full block. Whipstitch 4 hexagons to a center hexagon to make a partial block.

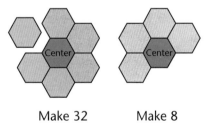

Make 32   Make 8

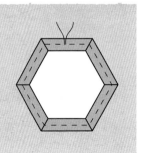

NOTE: In traditional English paper piecing, the seam allowances are basted by hand with a needle and thread. I don't do this, but feel free to do so if you prefer.

2. Repeat step 1 with the diamonds. Sew 6 diamonds to each full block, and 3 diamonds to each partial block.

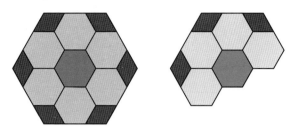

Assembling and Finishing the Quilt

I. Lay out the Hexagon blocks in a pleasing color arrangement, in 8 rows of 4 full blocks with 1 partial block at the end of each row. Alternate the placement of the partial blocks from row to row as shown below.

2. Finger-press the seam allowance over the freezer-paper triangles. With right sides facing and edges aligned, whipstitch the triangles to the sides of the Hexagon blocks.

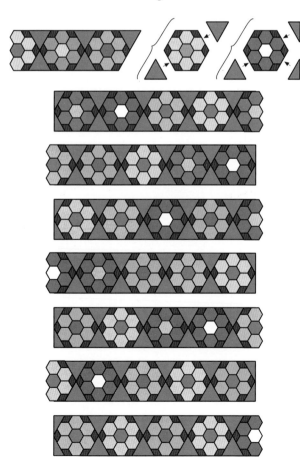

3. Whipstitch the rows together.
4. Use a long ruler and a rotary cutter to straighten the sides of the quilt. Place the ¼" line on the ruler in the middle of the hexagons on the partial blocks, and on the tips of the black diamonds on the full blocks. Trim along the edge of the ruler.

5. Measure, cut, and sew the 1½"-wide inner-border strips to the quilt top, referring to "Straight-Cut Borders" on pages 77–78. Repeat with the 4½"-wide outer-border strips.
6. Remove the freezer-paper templates.
7. Refer to "Finishing Techniques" on pages 79–83. Layer quilt top with batting and backing; baste. Quilt as desired or follow the quilting suggestion. Bind the edges of the quilt.

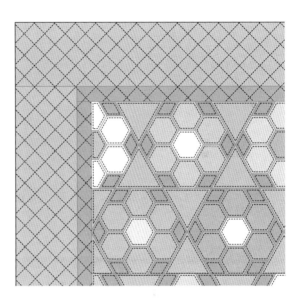

8. Label your quilt.

Antique Quilt

Elongated Hexagon

Quilt Size: 72" x 82"

Color photo on page 33

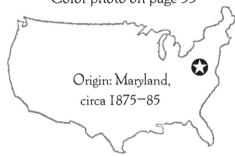

Origin: Maryland,
circa 1875–85

Construction: The quilt was hand pieced and hand quilted. The border was added by machine and the back of the quilt was turned to the front to finish the edges.

The one-patch pattern used in this quilt is an elongated hexagon. Most of the quilt reference books identify this pattern as a Honeycomb or Honeycomb Patch. This puzzles me, because a true honeycomb shape, or hexagon, has six equal sides.

"Elongated Hexagon" is a wonderful example of a charm quilt. Charm quilts make rich study pieces for textile historians. Since no two fabrics are alike, they can offer an extensive look at the fabrics used by early quiltmakers.

New Quilt

Blooms! Blooms! Blooms!

Quilt Size: 94½" x 97¼"

The Trip Around the World setting can be used with scrap fabrics as the antique quilt shows so beautifully. We used floral fabrics for our Trip Around the World, which was fun for two quilting and gardening friends to piece together. Nature's blooms work together to create beauty in our gardens, in wildflower meadows, and in your quilt.

A flannel design wall—permanent or temporary—makes the designing of this quilt much easier. Place the hexagons on the wall as you cut to make certain the fabrics create a pleasing arrangement.

Materials: 44"-wide fabric

1⅝ yds.	Fabric 1
1½ yds.	Fabric 2
1⅜ yds.	Fabric 3
1⅜ yds.	Fabric 4
1¼ yds.	Fabric 5
1⅜ yds.	Fabric 6
1½ yds.	Fabric 7
1⅝ yds.	Fabric 8
1⅞ yds.	Fabric 9
½ yd. for inner border	
2⅞ yds. for outer border	
8½ yds. for backing	
¾ yd. for binding	
Template plastic	

(Cutting instructions continued on page 38)

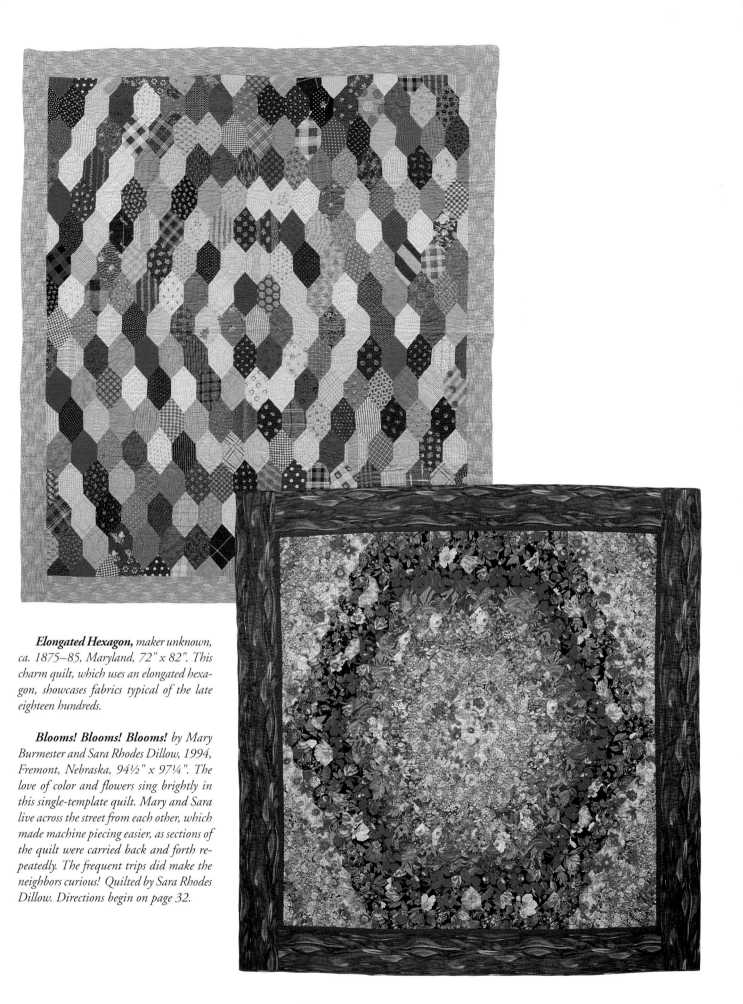

Elongated Hexagon, *maker unknown, ca. 1875–85, Maryland, 72" x 82". This charm quilt, which uses an elongated hexagon, showcases fabrics typical of the late eighteen hundreds.*

Blooms! Blooms! Blooms! *by Mary Burmester and Sara Rhodes Dillow, 1994, Fremont, Nebraska, 94½" x 97¼". The love of color and flowers sing brightly in this single-template quilt. Mary and Sara live across the street from each other, which made machine piecing easier, as sections of the quilt were carried back and forth repeatedly. The frequent trips did make the neighbors curious! Quilted by Sara Rhodes Dillow. Directions begin on page 32.*

33 · Quilt Gallery

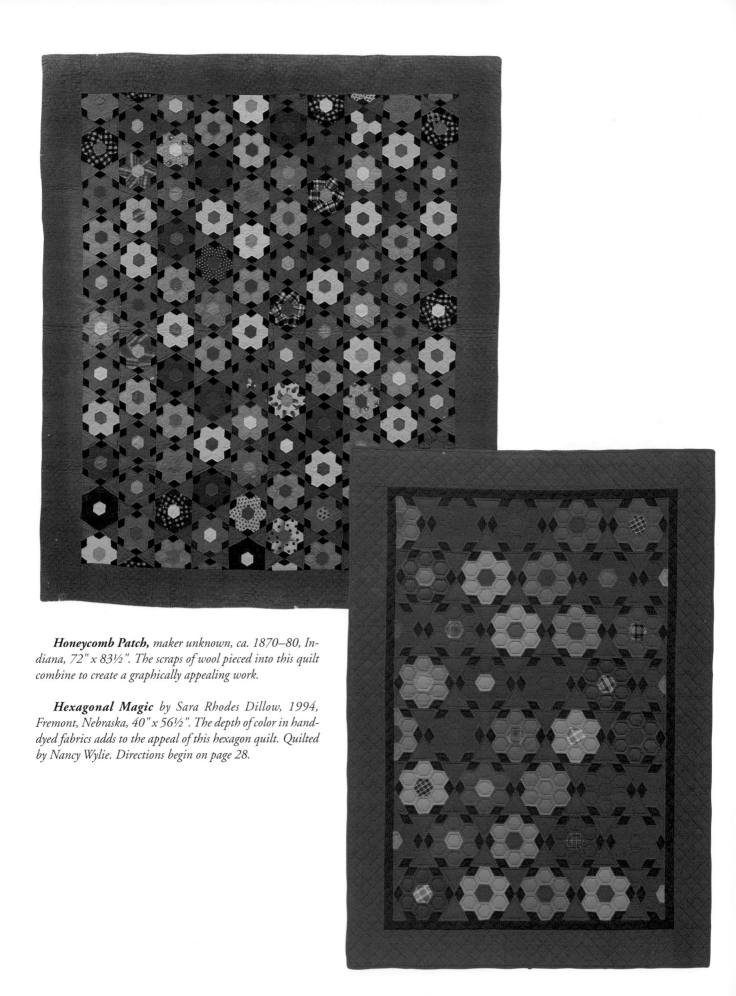

Honeycomb Patch, maker unknown, ca. 1870–80, Indiana, 72" x 83½". The scraps of wool pieced into this quilt combine to create a graphically appealing work.

Hexagonal Magic by Sara Rhodes Dillow, 1994, Fremont, Nebraska, 40" x 56½". The depth of color in hand-dyed fabrics adds to the appeal of this hexagon quilt. Quilted by Nancy Wylie. Directions begin on page 28.

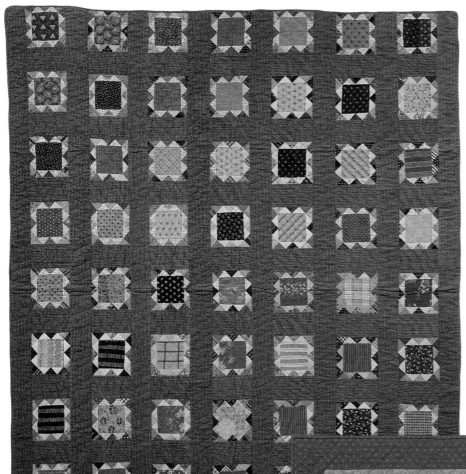

Framed Square, *maker unknown, ca. 1875–85, Douglas County, Nebraska, 70" x 83". An anonymous quiltmaker shares the treasures of the scrapbag in this fabric showcase.*

Fireside Fantasy *by June Vogltance, 1994, Dodge, Nebraska, 50½" x 58½". The colors of this wall quilt reflect the warmth of hearth and home. Directions begin on page 40.*

Broken Dishes Strippy, *maker unknown, ca. 1875–1900, New Hampshire, 61" x 89½". A vibrant plaid showcases Broken Dishes blocks. The pieced blocks exhibit a variety of period fabrics.*

The Dishes Are Done *by Sara Rhodes Dillow, 1994, Fremont, Nebraska, 60¼" x 55". The strips of Broken Dishes blocks appear to float over the alternating floral-and-vine fabric. Quilted by Alberta Nickols. Directions begin on page 43.*

Quilt Plan

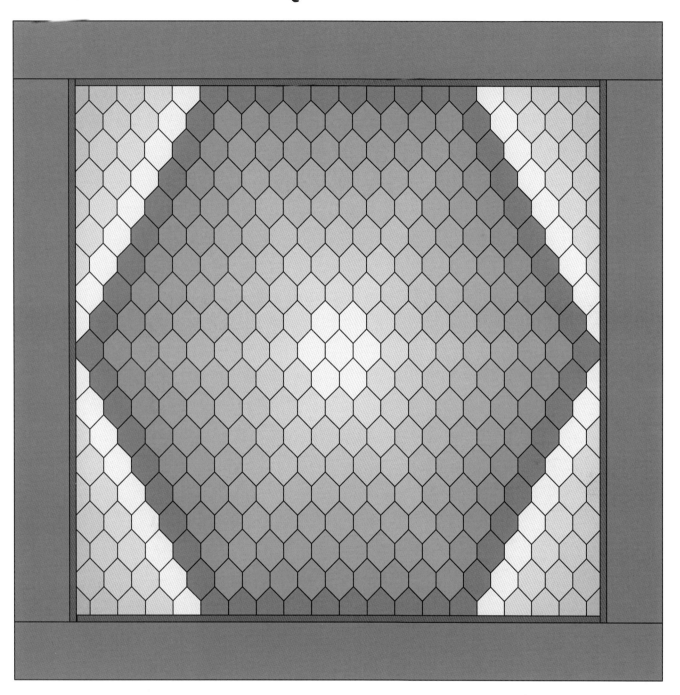

Cutting

Use the template on page 86.

From floral fabrics, cut:

To make the Trip Around the World design shown in the quilt on page 33, cut the following number of hexagons for each row. See "Cutting and Piecing Hexagons" below.

Fabric 1	Center		1
Fabric 1	Row	1	6
Fabric 2	Row	2	12
Fabric 3	Row	3	18
Fabric 4	Row	4	24
Fabric 5	Row	5	30
Fabric 6	Row	6	36
Fabric 7	Row	7	42
Fabric 8	Row	8	48
Fabric 9	Row	9	54
Fabric 1	Row	10	36
Fabric 2	Row	11	28
Fabric 3	Row	12	20
Fabric 4	Row	13	12
Fabric 5	Row	14	4

From the inner-border fabric, cut the following strips across the width of the fabric (crosswise grain):

8 strips, each 1½" x 42"

From the outer-border fabric, cut the following strips from the lengthwise grain of the fabric:

2 strips, each 8½" x 80", for top and bottom borders

2 strips, each 8½" x 99", for side borders

From the fabric for binding, cut:

10 strips, each 2¼" x 42"

Assembling the Quilt

The hexagons can be machine pieced if you and your sewing machine are friends! Handpiecing is pleasant, however, and these hexagons make a great take-along project.

I. Arrange hexagons on your design wall. Join the hexagons in short diagonal rows.

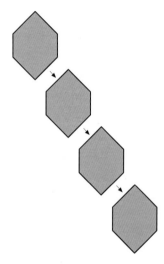

Cutting and Piecing Hexagons

Try this method for piecing the hexagons, by hand or machine. Make a plastic template of the elongated hexagon (template on page 86). Trace around the hexagon on the wrong side of the fabric. Cut the fabric out, adding a ¼"-wide seam allowance (you can eyeball this amount) all around the drawn shape. To join two hexagons, pin them together with right sides facing, matching the pencil lines on the pieces. Stitch only on the pencil line, starting and stopping at the seam intersection.

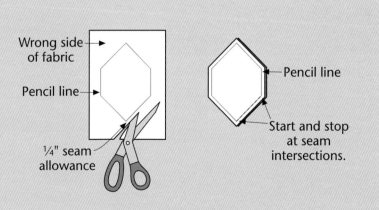

Wrong side of fabric

Pencil line

¼" seam allowance

Pencil line

Start and stop at seam intersections.

2. Sew the short diagonal rows together to make a section. Then join the sections.

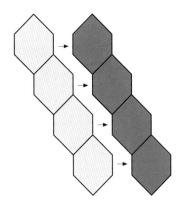

3. Use a long ruler and a rotary cutter to straighten the edges of the quilt. For the sides, place the ¼" line on the ruler on the middle of the hexagons as shown. For the top and bottom edges, place the edge of the ruler on the intersection between 2 hexagons. Trim along the edge of the ruler.

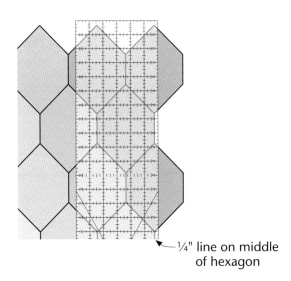

¼" line on middle of hexagon

Edge of ruler on intersection

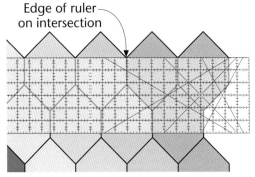

Finishing the Quilt

1. Referring to "Borders with Straight-Cut Corners" on page 77–78, measure, cut, and sew the 1½"-wide inner-border strips to the top and bottom edges of the quilt top first, then to the sides. Repeat with the 8½"-wide outer-border strips.

2. Refer to "Finishing Techniques" on pages 79–83. Layer the quilt top with batting and backing; baste. Quilt as desired, or follow one of the quilting suggestions. Bind the edges of the quilt.

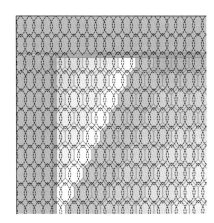

Quilting suggestion from original quilt

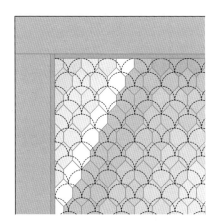

Quilting suggestion from Blooms! Blooms! Blooms!

3. Label your quilt.

Antique Quilt

Framed Square

Quilt Size: 70" x 83"

Color photo on page 35

Origin: Douglas County, Nebraska,
circa 1875–1900

Construction: This antique quilt was machine pieced and hand quilted. It has an applied binding, and a brown plaid was used for the backing.

This is a simple block design. It is mysterious that no mention of it is found in any of the quilt reference books. The simplicity of the pattern would almost ensure its popularity. The design is similar to the first triangle border around the center square of the Our Village Green and Corn and Beans blocks.

Do you know the name of this block? Until the real name is revealed, I'll just refer to it as the "Framed Square." Since there are no rules for naming a new quilt block, quiltmakers can use "quilters' license" and refer to blocks with the names of their choice. It will be interesting to see if the names we use for quilt blocks today undergo a transformation, since we give the quilts we make such fancy names. Will a block take on the name of the quilt and gradually lose its original identity?

Scrap quilts, like charm quilts, provide wonderful examples of the textiles that were available to quiltmakers when the quilt was made. This scrap quilt contains a variety of fabric designs, including leaves, small florals, and geometrics.

New Quilt

Fireside Fantasy

Quilt Size: 50½" x 58½"

Finished Block Size: 6"

The center square of this block can be a showcase for floral or geometric prints. The triangles around the center block should contrast in value to create a frame that shows off the center square.

Materials: 44"-wide fabric

⅝ yd. total assorted feature fabrics for center square
⅝ yd. total assorted light fabrics for light triangles
1 yd. total assorted dark fabrics for dark triangles
1⅝ yds. tan for sashing and inner border
2 yds. red for outer border
3¼ yds. for backing
½ yd. for binding

Cutting

Measurements include ¼"-wide seam allowances.

(Cutting instructions continued on page 42)

Quilt Plan

Color Key

Feature fabrics

Lights

Darks

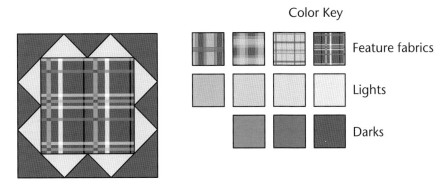

Framed Square

From assorted feature fabrics, cut:
30 squares, each 4½" x 4½"

From assorted light fabrics, cut:
60 squares*, each 3¼" x 3¼"; cut the squares twice diagonally to yield 240 small triangles

*Within each block, the same print is used for the light triangles. Cut at least two 3¼" squares from each light fabric.

From assorted dark fabrics, cut:
30 squares*, each 3¼" x 3¼"; cut the squares twice diagonally to yield 120 small triangles
60 squares*, each 2⅞" x 2⅞"; cut the squares once diagonally to yield 120 large triangles

*Within each block, the same print is used for the dark triangles. Cut at least one 3¼" square and two 2⅞" squares from each dark fabric.

From tan fabric, cut the following strips from the lengthwise grain:
4 strips, each 2½" x 46½", for vertical sashing
3 strips, each 2½" x 52"; crosscut into 24 strips, each 2½" x 6½", for horizontal sashing strips. Cut one additional strip, 2½" x 6½", from leftovers, for a total of 25 horizontal sashing strips.
2 strips, each 2½" x 46", for inner top and bottom borders
2 strips, each 2½" x 54", for inner side borders

From red fabric, cut the following strips from the lengthwise grain:
2 strips, each 4½" x 54", for outer top and bottom borders
2 strips, each 4½" x 62", for outer side borders

From fabric for binding, cut:
6 strips, each 2¼" x 42"

Assembling the Blocks

I. Use 8 matching small light triangles and 4 matching small dark triangles to make 4 side units for each block.

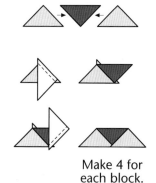

Make 4 for each block.

2. Sew 4 matching side units to each 4½" center square. Add 4 matching large dark triangles to the corners to complete a Framed Square block.

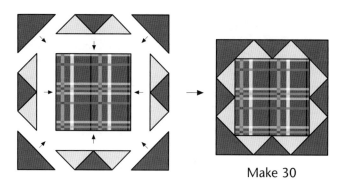

Make 30

Assembling and Finishing the Quilt

I. Arrange the blocks in 5 vertical rows of 6 blocks each, with horizontal sashing strips between the blocks. Sew the blocks and sashing strips together.

2. Sew the rows of blocks together with vertical sashing strips between the rows.

3. Sew each 2½"-wide top inner-border strip to a 4½"-wide top outer-border strip. Treat the resulting unit as a single border strip. Repeat with the bottom and side borders. Measure, cut, and sew the border strips to the quilt top, referring to "Borders with Mitered Corners" on pages 78–79.

4. Refer to "Finishing Techniques" on pages 79–83. Layer your quilt top with batting and backing; baste. Quilt as desired or follow the quilting suggestion. Bind the edges of the quilt.

5. Label your quilt.

Antique Quilt

Broken Dishes Strippy

Quilt Size: 61" x 89½"
Color photo on page 36

Origin: New Hampshire,
circa 1875–1900

Construction: This antique quilt was hand pieced and hand quilted. It has an applied binding.

Strippy quilts have been made since the early eighteen hundreds. They were often made as quick-pieced utility quilts or as a showcase for a favorite fabric. It was also a good way to use fabric scraps and stretch showy fabrics that might have been in short supply. Strippy quilts generally were made of an uneven number of pieced strips.

Have you ever tried to explain the name of a quilt block to a nonquilter? Broken Dishes is a challenging name to account for! It is fun to imagine the quiltmaker who, once upon a time while wiping the supper dishes, dropped a dish (we all know that it would have been her favorite serving bowl) and saw a block design created by the broken pieces on the floor. The quilter probably threw the towel down and made a mad dash for her sewing basket or piecing pocket. The quilt block would have made the best of an unhappy situation.

New Quilt

The Dishes Are Done

Quilt Size: 60¼" x 55"
Finished Block Size: 3½"

Materials: 44"-wide fabric

1⅜ yds. green for blocks
1⅜ yds. cream for blocks
1 yd. pink for strippy setting
3⅛ yds. blue for sashings and borders
3½ yds. for backing
½ yd. for binding

(Instructions continued on page 45)

Quilt Plan

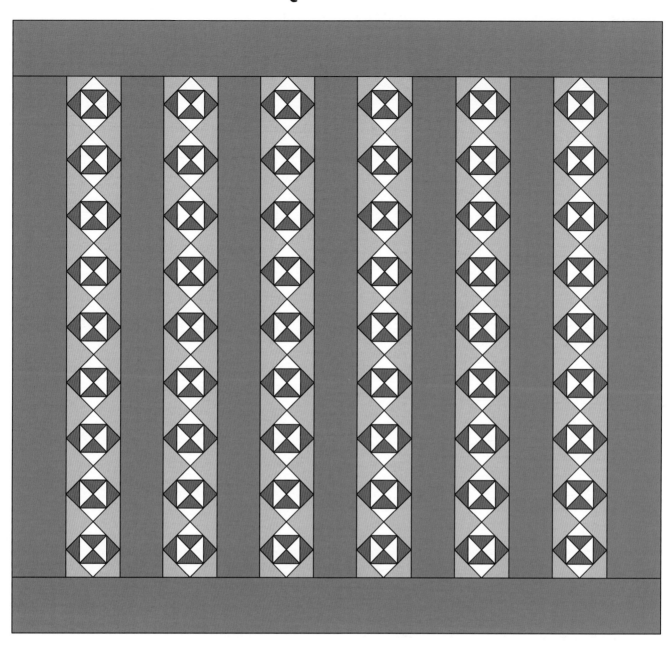

Color Key

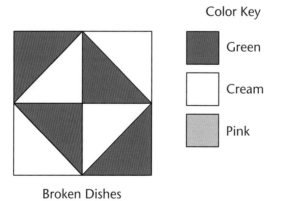

Broken Dishes

Cutting

All measurements include ¼"-wide seam allowances. Cut strips across the width of the fabric (crosswise grain) unless otherwise instructed.

From green fabric, cut:
  4 pieces, each 11" x 40", for bias squares

From cream fabric, cut:
  4 pieces, each 11" x 40", for bias squares

From pink fabric, cut:
  4 strips, each 6¼"; crosscut into 24 squares, each 6¼" x 6¼". Cut squares twice diagonally to yield 96 side triangles
  1 strip, 3⅜"; crosscut into 12 squares, each 3⅜" x 3⅜". Cut the squares once diagonally to yield 24 corner triangles.

From blue fabric, cut the following strips from the lengthwise grain:
  5 strips, each 4½" x 46", for sashings
  2 strips, each 5½" x 46", for side borders
  2 strips, each 5½" x 62", for top and bottom borders

From fabric for binding, cut:
  6 strips, each 2¼" x 42"

Assembling the Blocks

I. Use the 11" x 40" pieces of cream and green fabrics to make bias squares, referring to the instructions on pages 74–75. From each pair of cream and green fabrics, cut a total of 16 bias strips and make 2 bias-strip units, each with a total of 8 bias strips, alternating the light and dark strips.

  Cut the bias strips 2¼" wide
  Cut the segments 2¼" wide
  Cut a total of 216 bias squares, 2¼" x 2¼"

2. Sew 4 bias squares together to make a Broken Dishes block.

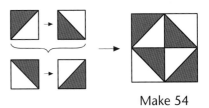

Make 54

Assembling and Finishing the Quilt

I. Arrange the blocks and side and corner triangles into 6 vertical rows of 9 blocks each. Sew the blocks and triangles together into diagonal rows as shown below. Press the seams toward the triangles. Join the diagonal rows.

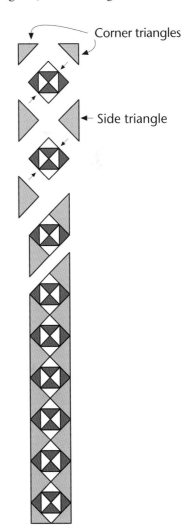

Make 6 rows.

2. Measure the length of the vertical rows and trim the sashing strips to that measurement. Sew the rows of blocks and sashing strips together.

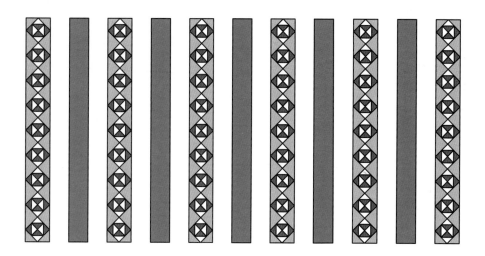

3. Measure, cut, and sew the 5½"-wide border strips to the quilt top, referring to "Straight-Cut Borders" on pages 77–78.

4. Refer to "Finishing Techniques" on pages 79–83. Layer quilt top with batting and backing; baste. Quilt as desired or follow the quilting suggestion. Bind the edges of the quilt.

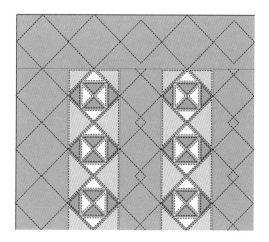

5. Label your quilt.

Antique Quilt

Rolling Star

Quilt Size: 72" x 82"

Color photo on page 54

Origin: Holton, Kansas,

circa 1880–1900

Construction: This quilt was hand quilted and hand pieced, and the front was turned to the back to finish the edges.

I love the sophisticated colors of this quilt! Pink-and-green has long been a favorite color combination, even in the nineteenth century, as evidenced by this quilt. The pink used for the squares was called "double pink" fabric and was available throughout the last half of the eighteen hundreds. Double pink fabric is found in many scrap quilts of this period.

Celestial inspirations are visible in some of the earliest American quilts. Rolling Star is just one of an extremely large number of star patterns. The block name suggests a star moving across a velvety night sky, or perhaps a much faster moving star, a falling star.

New Quilt

Star Garden

Quilt Size: 55¾" x 55¾"

Finished Block Size: Rolling Star, 12", LeMoyne Star, 4"

Materials: 44"-wide fabric

¾ yd. dark blue for blocks and inner border
½ yd. light green for blocks
½ yd. dark green for blocks
½ yd. pink for blocks
⅝ yd. yellow for blocks
1¾ yds. floral for sashings and outer border
3½ yds. for backing
½ yd. for binding
Template plastic

Cutting

Measurements include ¼"-wide seam allowances. Cut all strips across the width of the fabric (crosswise grain) unless otherwise instructed. Use the templates on page 86.

From dark blue fabric, cut:
    3 strips, each 2¼" x 42", for Rolling Star blocks
    6 strips, each 1½" x 42", for inner border
    32 of Template 3 for LeMoyne Star blocks

From light green fabric, cut:
    3 strips, each 2¼" x 42", for Rolling Star blocks
    32 of Template 3 for LeMoyne Star blocks

(Cutting instructions continued on page 49)

Quilt Plan

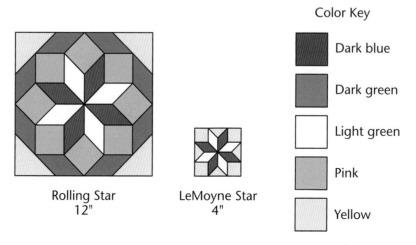

Rolling Star
12"

LeMoyne Star
4"

Color Key

■ Dark blue

■ Dark green

□ Light green

■ Pink

■ Yellow

From dark green fabric, cut:

6 strips, each 2¼" x 42", for Rolling Star blocks

From pink fabric, cut:

4 strips, each 3" x 42"; crosscut into 56 squares, each 3" x 3", for Rolling Star blocks

1 strip, 3⅜" x 42"; crosscut into 8 squares, each 3⅜" x 3⅜". Cut the squares once diagonally to yield 16 half-square triangles for Rolling Star half- and quarter-blocks.

From yellow fabric, cut:

2 strips, each 4⅜" x 42"; crosscut into 12 squares, each 4⅜" x 4⅜". Cut the squares once diagonally to yield 24 half-square triangles for Rolling Star block corners.

1 strip, 3⅜" x 42"; crosscut into 8 squares, each 3⅜" x 3⅜". Cut the squares once diagonally to yield 16 half-square triangles for Rolling Star half- and quarter-blocks.

24 of Template 1 for LeMoyne Star blocks

48 of Template 2 for LeMoyne Star blocks

From floral fabric, cut the following strips from the lengthwise grain:

4 strips, each 4½" x 58", for outer borders

16 strips, each 4½" x 12½", for sashing

From fabric for binding, cut:

6 strips, each 2¼" x 42"

Assembling the Rolling Star Blocks

1. Trim the selvage ends of the 2¼"-wide strips at a 45° angle. To cut the diamonds, place a rotary-cutting ruler's 45° angle at the edge of the strip and the 2¼" mark on the ruler at the cut edge of the strip. Cut a total of 32 dark blue diamonds, 32 light green diamonds, and 64 green diamonds.

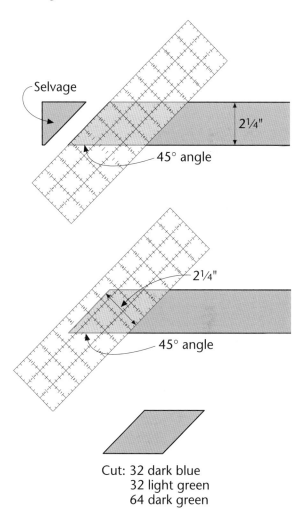

Cut: 32 dark blue
32 light green
64 dark green

2. Mark seam intersections on the wrong side of the dark blue and light green diamonds.

3. Arrange the diamonds in a star, alternating the colors. Sew the dark blue and light green diamonds into pairs. Begin stitching at the raw edge in the center and stop at the ¼" mark at the point of the diamond; backstitch. Press all seams in the same direction.

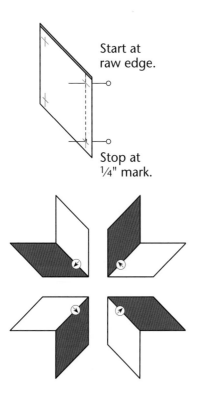

4. Sew 2 diamond pairs together in the same manner to make a half-star.
5. Pin the star halves together, matching the center and points carefully. Stitch from ¼" mark to ¼" mark; backstitch.

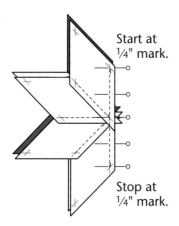

6. Set in 8 pink corner squares. Mark the seam allowance intersections on the squares. With right sides together, pin one corner of a square to the inside corner between two diamonds. Align the raw edges of the square and the diamond, matching the intersection marks. Stitch from the mark at the inside corner to the mark at the other end; backstitch at the beginning and end of the seam.

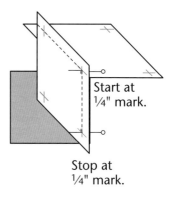

7. Pin the square to the adjacent diamond, matching the seam allowance intersection marks. Stitch from mark to mark; backstitch at both ends.

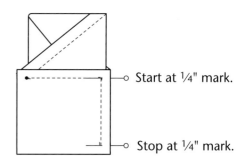

8. Mark the seam intersection on the wrong side of the green diamonds. Sew 8 dark green diamonds to the center star, between each of the pink squares. Stitch from the ¼" mark to the raw edge.

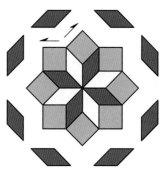

9. Sew a yellow corner triangle to each of the 4 corners to complete the Rolling Star block.

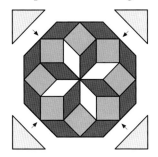

Make 5

10. Refer to steps 1–8 above, and follow the piecing diagrams below to make half-blocks and quarter-blocks.

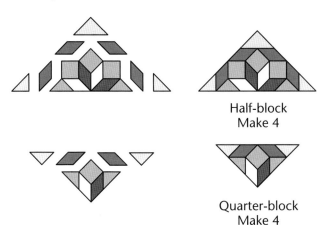

Half-block
Make 4

Quarter-block
Make 4

Assembling the LeMoyne Stars

Piece 4 LeMoyne Stars and 8 LeMoyne Half-stars, referring to steps 2–5 on pages 49–50. Refer to steps 6–7 for setting-in the squares and triangles.

Make 4   Make 8

Assembling and Finishing the Quilt

1. Arrange the blocks and sashing strips in diagonal rows as shown at right. Sew the rows together. Press the seams toward the sashing strips.

2. Join the rows.
3. Join the 1½"-wide inner-border strips end-to-end to make one long strip and crosscut 4 strips, each 50" long. Sew each inner-border strip to a 4½"-wide outer-border strip and treat the resulting unit as a single strip. Measure, cut, and sew the border strips to the quilt top, referring to "Borders with Mitered Corners" on pages 78–79.
4. Refer to "Finishing Techniques" on pages 79–83. Layer your quilt top with batting and backing; baste. Quilt as desired or follow the quilting suggestion. Bind edges of the quilt.

5. Label your quilt.

Antique Quilt

Log Cabin Medallion

Quilt Size: 74" x 74"
Color photo on page 53

Origin: New Hampshire,
circa 1875–1900

Construction: This quilt was hand pieced and was most likely used in summer, since it contains no batting and was not quilted. The front fabric was turned to the back to finish the quilt edges.

This scrap quilt contains a nice selection of the conversation prints that were common in the last quarter of the nineteenth century. Conversation prints feature realistic designs of common objects, such as horseshoes, pins, and stars.

Among the many fabrics are six different double-pink prints.

I often feel that quiltmakers of years ago were telling stories through their quilts. In the story I have made up for this quilt, there is a snug log cabin built in a clearing in the woods, represented by the center medallion of four Log Cabin blocks.

The first border of Flying Geese may represent the quiltmaker's own flock of geese and chickens, or perhaps they are the images of the flocks of wild geese winging over the cabin in their migratory pattern. A blueberry print was used in the corners of the Flying Geese border. Could this be the quiltmaker's blueberry patch? The floral fabric used in the second border could be a reminder of a garden, and the triangles in the third border could be the fence that surrounds the log cabin.

Our pioneer family probably felt secure in their home, but they were aware of danger lurking in the woods. The Bear's Paw blocks may be symbols of an ever present danger.

(Refer to "Bears in the Woods" on pages 57–62.)

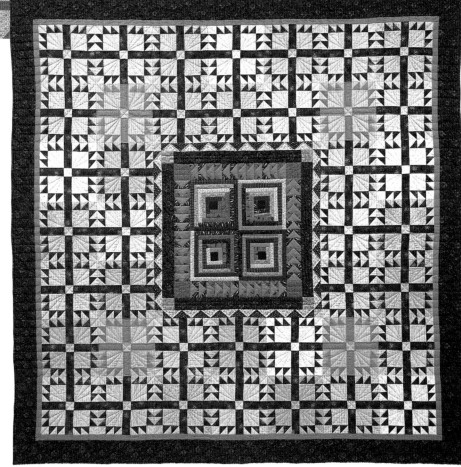

Log Cabin Medallion, *maker unknown, ca. 1875–1900, New Hampshire, 74" x 74". The fabrics in this medallion quilt present a subdued palette. Because it consists of a top and a back with no batting or quilting, this quilt was probably meant for summer use.*

Bears in the Woods *by Jean Gausman, 1994, Fremont, Nebraska, 84" x 84". This medallion quilt features the longtime favorite Log Cabin block as the focal point. A secondary pattern develops in the Bear's Paw blocks. Directions begin on page 57.*

Rolling Star *maker unknown, ca. 1880–1900, Holton, Kansas, 72" x 82". Eight-pointed stars pieced in pink, green, and blue reflect a popular color scheme.*

Star Garden *by Sara Rhodes Dillow, 1994, Fremont, Nebraska, 55¾" x 55¾". Stars shine in this delicate interpretation of a fabric flower garden. Directions begin on page 47.*

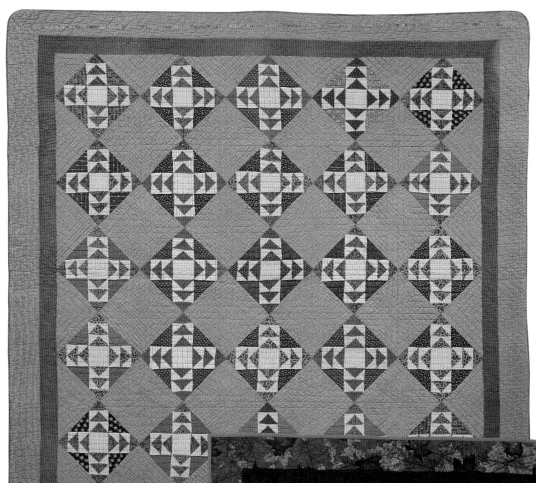

Toad in a Puddle, *maker unknown, ca. 1900–1925, Nebraska, 73½" x 76". An assortment of red fabrics brightens this quilt, which appears to have provided warmth on many a winter night.*

Drifting Leaves *by Judy McClure, 1994, Omaha, Nebraska, 61½" x 61½". Judy's outline quilting enhances the leaves drifting across this quilt. Spider webs quilted in metallic thread make the surface sparkle. Directions begin on page 63.*

Nebraska Block Quilt, *maker unknown, 1924, Saunders County, Nebraska, 75" x 76". Red, white, and blue fabrics and a state block pattern give this quilt a patriotic feeling.*

Amber Waves of Grain *by Kathy Murphy, 1994, Fremont, Nebraska, 53" x 53". Reflecting the colors of a bountiful harvest, this Nebraska block quilt is appropriate for a state that is an agricultural giant. Directions begin on page 67.*

Quilt Gallery · 56

Quilt Plan

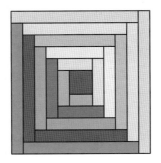

Log Cabin Block

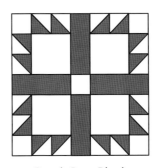

Bear's Paw Block

Bears in the Woods

Quilt Size: 84" x 84"

(Refer to "Log Cabin Medallion" on page 52.)

Notice that the Bear's Paw blocks look quite different in the two quilts. In the new quilt, the position of the lights and darks was changed slightly, creating an interesting design across the surface of the quilt.

Materials: 44"-wide fabric

Log Cabin Blocks
⅜ yd. total assorted dark fabrics
⅜ yd. total assorted light fabrics

Flying Geese Border
¼ yd. yellow
⅛ yd. dark yellow for corner squares
¼ yd. dark fabric

Floral Border
⅜ yd. floral print
⅛ yd. light fabric for corner squares

Triangle Border
¼ yd. dark fabric
¼ yd. light #1
⅛ yd. light #2 for corner squares

Bear's Paw Blocks
¾ yd. each of 7 different light fabrics
⅝ yd. yellow
3¼ yds. dark fabric
½ yd. for inner border
1¼ yds. for outer border
7½ yds. for backing
⅔ yd. for binding

Cutting and Assembling
Log Cabin Blocks

Finished block size: 9"

From assorted dark fabrics, cut:
4 squares, each 2" x 2", for center
Approximately 235" of 1¼"-wide strips

From assorted light fabrics, cut:
Approximately 265" of 1¼"-wide strips

I. Sew the strips in a clockwise direction around the center square. You can make all the Log Cabin blocks the same or make them different. For each block, begin by placing the center square on the first dark strip. If you are making all the blocks the same, stitch the remaining 3 center squares to the first dark strip. If you are making them all different, sew each center square to a different dark strip. Stitch ¼" from the edge. Trim the excess strip and press the seam toward log #1. Place the unit on the second dark strip with log #1 closest to you as you stitch the unit to the second strip. Trim the excess fabric and press the seams toward log #2. Place the unit on the first light strip (log #3); stitch, trim, and press the seams toward log #3. Place the unit on the second light strip (log #4); stitch, trim, and press the seams toward log #4. Continue adding logs around the block, alternating 2 dark strips and 2 light strips, until you have 5 rows of logs around the center square.

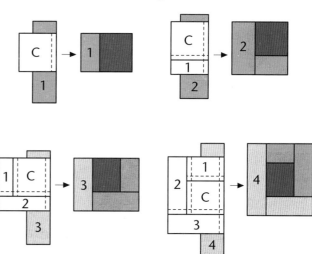

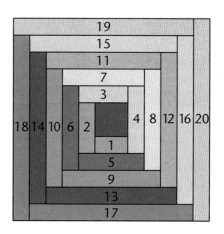

2. Sew the 4 Log Cabin blocks together.

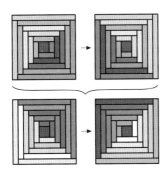

Cutting and Assembling the Flying Geese Border

From yellow fabric, cut:
 2 strips, each 3" x 42"; crosscut into 24 squares, each 3" x 3"; cut the squares once diagonally to yield 48 half-square triangles

From dark yellow fabric, cut:
 4 squares, each 3½" x 3½"

From dark fabric, cut:
 3 strips, each 2⅜" x 42"; crosscut into 48 squares, each 2⅜" x 2⅜"; cut the squares once diagonally to yield 96 half-square triangles

I. Sew 2 small, dark triangles to a large, yellow triangle.

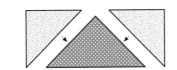

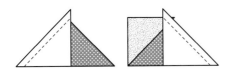

Make 48

2. Join 12 Flying Geese units to make a border strip. Make 4 border strips.

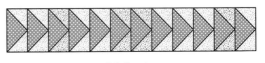

Make 4

3. Sew 2 Flying Geese border strips to the sides of the center Log Cabin blocks. Sew a dark yellow corner square to each end of the remaining Flying Geese border strips. Sew these to the top and bottom edges. Press seams toward the Log Cabin blocks.

Cutting and Assembling the Floral Border

From floral print, cut:
 4 strips, each 2½" x 24½"

From light fabric, cut:
 4 squares, each 2½" x 2½", for corner squares

I. Sew 2 floral border strips to the sides of the center unit. Sew a light corner square to each end of the remaining floral border strips. Sew these to the top and bottom edges of the center unit. Press the seams toward the floral border.

Cutting and Assembling the Triangle Border

From dark fabric, cut:

1 strip, 4¾" x 42"; crosscut into 7 squares, each 4¾" x 4¾". Cut the squares twice diagonally to yield 28 quarter-square triangles.

4 squares, each 2⅝" x 2⅝"; cut the squares once diagonally to yield 8 half-square triangles

From light fabric #1, cut:

1 strip, 4¾" x 42"; crosscut into 8 squares, each 4¾" x 4¾". Cut the squares twice diagonally to yield 32 quarter-square triangles.

From light fabric #2, cut:

4 squares, each 2¼" x 2¼"

I. Sew 8 light triangles and 7 dark triangles together to make a border strip. Add a small, dark triangle to opposite ends of each strip.

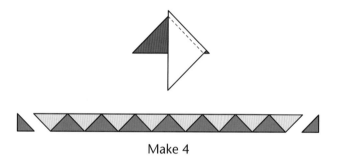

Make 4

2. Sew a border strip to opposite sides of the center unit. Sew a corner square to each end of the remaining border strips. Sew these to the top and bottom edges.

Cutting and Assembling the Bear's Paw Blocks

Finished Block Size: 10½"

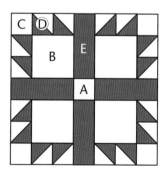

NOTE: The cutting directions that follow are for making 36 light-and-dark blocks and 4 light-and-yellow blocks. If you prefer to make all the blocks the same, substitute dark fabric for the yellow fabric.

From each ¾-yard piece of light fabric, cut:

6 squares, each 2" x 2", for piece A (42 total; you will use only 40)

2 strips, each 3½" x 42"; crosscut into 24 squares, each 3½" x 3½", for piece B (168 total; you will use only 160)

1 strip, 2" x 42"; crosscut into 20 squares, each 2" x 2", for piece C. Cut 3 additional 2" squares from each light fabric (161 total; you will use only 160).

1 piece from 6 of the light fabrics, each 13" x 42", for bias squares (piece D). From the seventh fabric, cut one piece, 11" x 42", for the light-and-yellow bias squares.

From yellow fabric, cut

1 piece, 11" x 42", for light-and-yellow bias squares (piece D)

2 strips, each 2" x 42"; crosscut into 16 rectangles, each 2" x 5", for piece E

From dark fabric, cut:

6 pieces, each 13" x 42", for light-and-dark bias squares (piece D)

18 strips, each 2" x 42"; crosscut into 144 rectangles, each 2" x 5", for piece E

I. Use the 13" x 42" pieces of light and dark fabrics and the 11" x 42" pieces of light and yellow fabrics to make bias squares, following the directions on pages 74–75. From each pair of light and dark fabrics, cut a total of 18 bias strips, and make 2 bias-strip units, each with a total of 9 bias strips, alternating the light and dark strips. From the paired light and yellow fabrics, cut a total of 16 bias strips. Make 2 bias-strip units, each with a total of 8 bias strips, alternating the light and yellow strips.

Cut the bias strips 2⅛" wide
Cut the segments 2" wide
Cut a total of 576 light-and-dark bias squares, each 2" x 2"
Cut a total of 64 light-and-yellow bias squares, each 2" x 2"

2. Sew pieces A, B, C, D, and E together, following the piecing diagram to make a Bear's Paw block. Match the light fabric pieces within each block. Be sure the dark triangles in the bias squares are oriented as shown. Make 4 blocks, using pieces cut from light and yellow fabrics.

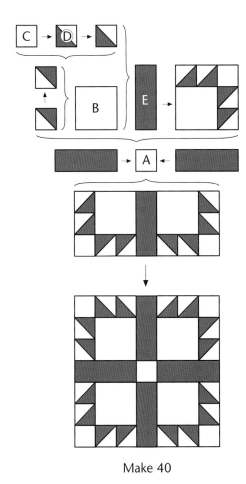

Make 40

Assembling and Finishing the Quilt

1. Sew the Bear's Paw blocks together in long rows and short rows as shown below. Sew 3 short rows together to make a side section. If you made 4 yellow blocks, be sure to position them as shown.

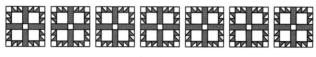

Make 2 rows.

Yellow blocks
Make 2 rows.

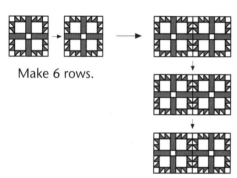

Make 6 rows.

Make 2

2. Sew the side sections to the sides of the center medallion. Add the long rows of blocks to the top and bottom edges.

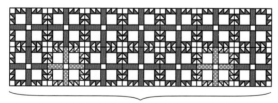

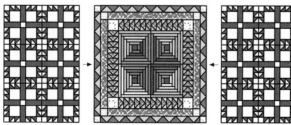

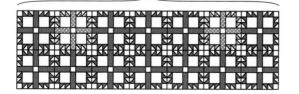

3. Cut 8 strips, each 1½" x 42", from the inner-border fabric. Cut 9 strips, each 4½" x 42", from the outer-border fabric.

4. Measure, cut, and sew the 1½"-wide inner-border strips to the quilt top, referring to "Straight-Cut Borders" on pages 77–78. Repeat with the 4½"-wide outer-border strips.

5. Refer to "Finishing Techniques" on pages 79–83. Layer your quilt top with batting and backing; baste. Quilt as desired or follow the quilting suggestion below. Cut 9 strips, each 2¼" x 42", from the fabric for binding, and bind the edges of the quilt.

6. Label your quilt.

Antique Quilt

Toad in a Puddle

Quilt Size: 73½" x 76"

Color photo on page 55

Origin: Nebraska,
circa 1900–1925

Construction: This quilt was hand pieced and hand quilted and has an applied binding.

Toad in a puddle
Happy as can be
World's in a muddle
But what care he?

Inspirations for quilt blocks and the resulting names never cease to amaze me. "Toad in a Puddle" is a name of the "you should have been there" type. Could the center square represent the toad and the triangles moving away from the center represent the ripples in the water in the puddle? Intriguing thought!

This quilt has seen better days. However, its charm seems to rest in having been used and enjoyed. Textile works are fragile, but deterioration can be slowed by proper attention. The responsibility belongs to the collector to provide the best care possible for these delicate artifacts, whether they are antiques or newly made.

New Quilt

Drifting Leaves

Quilt Size: 61½" x 61½"
Finished Block Size: 8½"

Materials: 44"-wide fabric

⅝ yd. beige for blocks
1 yd. teal for blocks
1¾ yds. navy blue for blocks and inner border
2 yds. leaf print for alternate blocks, setting triangles, and outer border
4 yds. for backing
½ yd. for binding

Cutting

Measurements include ¼"-wide seam allowances. Cut all strips across the width of the fabric (crosswise grain) unless otherwise instructed.

From beige fabric, cut:
3 strips, each 5½" x 42"; crosscut into 16 squares, each 5½" x 5½". Cut the squares twice diagonally to yield 64 quarter-square triangles for piece D.

From teal fabric, cut:
2 strips, each 3½" x 42"; crosscut into 16 squares, each 3½" x 3½", for piece A

(Cutting instructions continued on page 65)

Quilt Plan

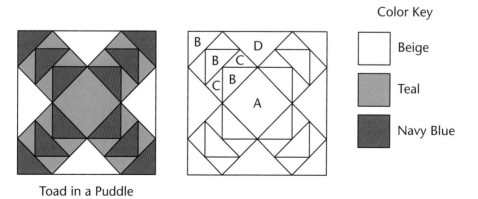

Toad in a Puddle

Color Key

⬜	Beige
🟩	Teal
🟦	Navy Blue

From the teal fabric, cut:
8 strips, each 2⅜" x 42"; crosscut into 128 squares, each 2⅜" x 2⅜". Cut squares once diagonally to yield 256 half-square triangles for piece C.

From the lengthwise grain of the navy blue fabric, cut:
4 strips, each 2¾" x 55", for inner borders
4 strips, each 4¼" x 52"; crosscut into 48 squares, each 4¼" x 4¼". Cut the squares twice diagonally to yield 192 quarter-square triangles for piece B.

From the lengthwise grain of the leaf print fabric, cut:
4 strips, each 4½" x 64", for outer borders
9 squares, each 9" x 9"
3 squares, each 13⅜" x 13⅜". Cut the squares twice diagonally to yield 12 quarter-square triangles for side triangles.
2 squares, each 6⅞" x 6⅞"; cut once diagonally to yield 4 half-square triangles for corner triangles

From fabric for binding, cut
6 strips, each 2¼" x 42"

Assembling the Blocks

I. Sew 2 small teal triangles (C) to a large navy blue triangle (B) to make a Flying Geese unit.

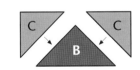

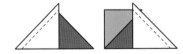

Make 128

2. Join 2 Flying Geese units and 1 navy blue triangle to make a Flying Geese section. Sew this unit to opposite sides of piece A.

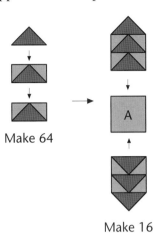

Make 64

Make 16

3. Sew 2 beige triangles (D) to the sides of each remaining Flying Geese section.

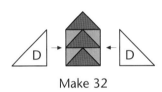

Make 32

4. Join the sections made in steps 2 and 3 to complete a Toad in a Puddle block.

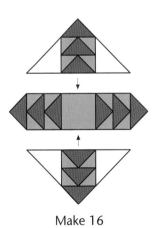

Make 16

Assembling and Finishing the Quilt

1. Arrange the plain and pieced blocks on point, adding side and corner triangles as shown below. Sew the blocks and side triangles in diagonal rows. Press the seams toward the plain blocks. Join the rows, matching the seams carefully. Add the corner triangles last.

2. Sew each 2¾"-wide inner-border strip to a 4½"-wide outer-border strip and treat the resulting unit as a single border strip. Measure, cut, and sew the border strips to the quilt top, referring to "Borders with Mitered Corners" on pages 78–79.

3. Refer to "Finishing Techniques" on pages 79–83. Layer quilt top with batting and backing; baste. Quilt as desired or follow the quilting suggestion. Bind the edges of the quilt.

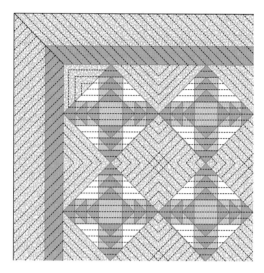

4. Label your quilt.

Antique Quilt

Nebraska Block Quilt

Quilt Size: 75" x 76"

Color photo on page 56

Origin: Saunders County,
Nebraska, 1924

Construction: This quilt was machine pieced and hand quilted, and has an applied binding.

In her "Encyclopedia of Pieced Quilt Patterns," Barbara Brackman credits "Hearth and Home" magazine, which was published from 1868 to 1933, with printing a variation of this block. "Chicago Tribune" quilt columnist Nancy Cabot (a pseudonym for Loretta Leitner Rising) is also credited with a 1933 Nebraska block that has a Ninepatch center.

The Nebraska quiltmaker had no way of knowing how appropriate the quilt's red-and-white color scheme would be in 1995, as fans of the Nebraska Cornhuskers celebrate the National Football Championship. The Cornhuskers wear scarlet and cream.

The Nebraska Block Quilt is a fine example of the importance of dating or documenting a quilt. The year "1924" is embroidered most emphatically on the outside border. A date prominently displayed thrills a quilt collector. History would be well served if the quiltmaker had added her name and community.

New Quilt

Amber Waves of Grain

Quilt Size: 53" x 53"

Finished Block Size: 12"

The variation of the Nebraska block that I used to make the new quilt is also referred to as Young Man's Fancy Variation in Judy Rehmel's reference work, *The Quilt I. D. Book.*

Materials: 44"-wide fabric

1⅝ yds. butterscotch
2⅝ yds. brown print
⅔ yd. purple
3¼ yds. for backing
½ yd. for binding

(Cutting instructions continued on page 69)

Quilt Plan

Color Key

Brown print

Purple

Butterscotch

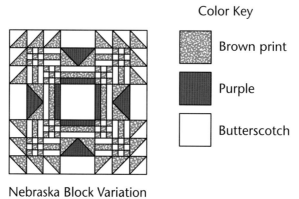

Nebraska Block Variation

Cutting

Measurements include ¼"-wide seam allowances. Cut all strips across the width of the fabric (crosswise grain).

From butterscotch fabric, cut:
    19 strips, each 1" x 42"
    3 strips, each 3½" x 42"; crosscut into 9 squares, each 3½" x 3½", for the center square, and 36 rectangles, each 2" x 3½"
    2 pieces, 11" x 42", for bias squares

From brown print fabric, cut:
    17 strips, each 1" x 42"
    2 strips, each 2⅜" x 42"; crosscut into 34 squares, each 2⅜" x 2⅜". Cut 2 additional 2⅜" squares from leftovers for a total of 36 squares. Cut the squares once diagonally to yield 72 half-square triangles.
    2 strips, each 3½" x 42½", for horizontal sashing strips
    2 strips, each 3½" x 42"; crosscut into 6 segments, each 3½" x 12½", for vertical sashing strips
    2 pieces, 11" x 42", for bias squares
    6 strips, each 4¾" x 42", for outer borders

From purple fabric, cut:
    3 strips, each 1" x 42"
    1 strip, 4¼" x 42"; crosscut into 9 squares, each 4¼" x 4¼". Cut the squares twice diagonally to yield 36 quarter-square triangles.
    5 strips, each 1¾" x 42", for inner borders

From fabric for binding cut:
    6 strips each 2¼" x 42"

Assembling the Blocks

I. Sew a 1" purple strip, a 1" brown strip, and a 1" butterscotch strip together to make a strip unit. Cut the strip units into a total of 36 segments, each 3½" wide.

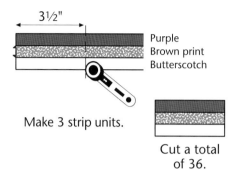

Make 3 strip units.

Cut a total of 36.

2. Sew a 1" butterscotch strip between two 1" brown strips to make a strip unit. Cut the strip units into a total of 144 segments, each 1" wide.

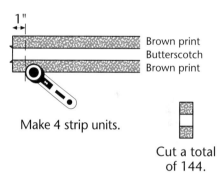

Make 4 strip units.

Cut a total of 144.

3. Sew a 1" brown strip between two 1" butterscotch strips to make a strip unit. Cut the strip units into a total of 72 segments, each 1" wide.

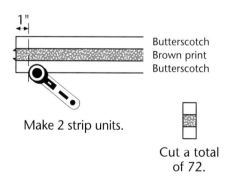

Make 2 strip units.

Cut a total of 72.

4. Join the segments from steps 2 and 3 to make a Ninepatch block.

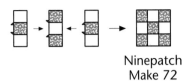

Ninepatch
Make 72

5. Sew a 1" brown strip between two 1" butterscotch strips to make a strip unit. Cut the strip units into a total of 72 segments, each 2" wide.

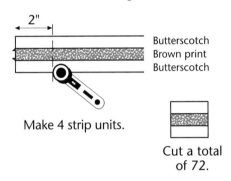

2"

Butterscotch
Brown print
Butterscotch

Make 4 strip units.

Cut a total
of 72.

6. Sew 2 small brown triangles to the sides of 1 large purple triangle.

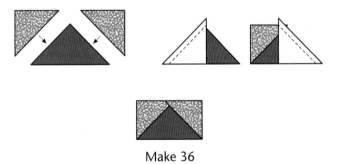

Make 36

7. Use the 11" x 42" pieces of butterscotch fabric and brown fabric to make bias squares, following the directions on pages 74–75. From each pair of fabrics, cut a total of 20 bias strips. Make 2 bias-strip units, using a total of 10 bias strips for each and alternating the butterscotch and brown fabrics.

Cut the bias strips 2⅛" wide
Cut the segments 2" wide
Cut a total of 180 bias squares, 2" x 2"

8. Assemble the units, following the piecing diagram below, to make a Nebraska block.

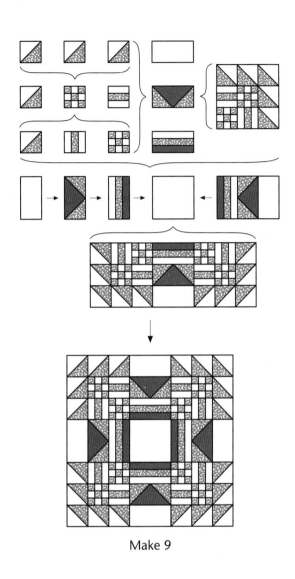

Make 9

Assembling and Finishing the Quilt

I. Sew 3 blocks and 2 vertical sashing strips together to make a block row.

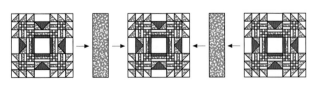

Make 3 rows.

2. Sew the rows and horizontal sashing strips together.

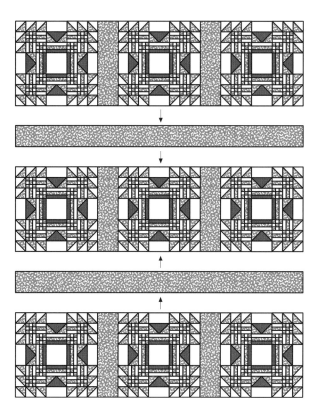

3. Measure, cut, and sew the 1¾"-wide border strips to the quilt top, referring to "Straight-Cut Borders" on pages 77–78. Repeat with 4¾"-wide outer-border strips.

4. Refer to "Finishing Techniques" on pages 79–83. Layer quilt top with batting and backing; baste. Quilt as desired or follow the quilting suggestion. Bind the edges of the quilt.

5. Label your quilt.

Quiltmaking Basics

This section covers quiltmaking techniques you need to use to assemble the quilts in this book.

Fabric Selection

Think how difficult it must have been to select fabrics fifty years ago when the choices were limited. It is a privilege to visit the quilt shops we have today and choose from the many luscious, colorful fabrics that are available.

One of the first considerations in making a quilt is fabric selection. You will spend many hours making a quilt; therefore, that expenditure of time deserves the best fabric you can buy. The fabric of choice is 100% cotton. Cotton holds its shape and is easy to handle.

Consider the quilt pattern you intend to make before selecting fabrics. Choose fabrics that contrast highly in value to show the designs to their best advantage. Select prints that are appropriate in size and scale for your pattern.

Preshrink all fabric to test for colorfastness and to remove excess dye. Wash dark and light colors separately so that dark colors do not run onto light fabrics. Iron fabrics so that you can cut them accurately.

Rotary Cutting

Instructions for quick-and-easy rotary cutting are provided wherever possible. All measurements include standard ¼"-wide seam allowances. For those unfamiliar with rotary-cutting techniques, a brief introduction is provided at right. For more information, see Donna Thomas's *Shortcuts: A Concise Guide to Rotary Cutting.*

To rotary-cut fabric:

1. Fold the fabric and match the selvages, aligning the crosswise and lengthwise grains as much as possible. Place the folded edge closest to you on the cutting mat.

2. To make a cut at a right angle to the fold, align a square ruler along the folded edge of the fabric. Place a long, straight ruler to the left of the square ruler, just covering the uneven raw edges of the left side of the fabric. Remove the square ruler and cut along the right edge of the ruler, rolling the rotary cutter away from you. Discard this strip. (Reverse this procedure if you are left-handed.)

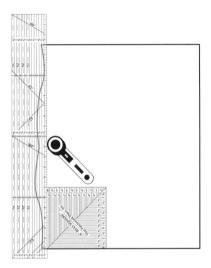

3. To cut strips, align the required measurement on the ruler with the newly cut edge of the fabric. For example, to cut a 3"-wide strip, place the 3" mark on the ruler on the edge of the fabric.

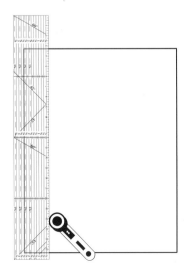

4. To cut squares and rectangles, cut strips in the required widths. Trim away the selvage ends of the strip. Align the required measurement on the ruler with the left edge of the strip and cut a square or rectangle. Continue cutting until you have the number of pieces needed.

Basic Piecing

Making Templates

The blocks in this book are designed for easy rotary-cutting and quick-piecing techniques. Some quilts, however, require the use of templates. Templates can be made from clear plastic or cardboard, but plastic templates are more durable and accurate. Since you can see through the plastic, it is easy to trace the templates accurately. You need only one template for each design in the quilt.

Place template plastic over each pattern piece and trace with a fine-line, permanent-ink marker. For appliqué templates, do not add seam allowances. Cut out the templates on the drawn lines. Templates for machine piecing include the required ¼"-wide seam allowance. Cut out the template on the outside line so that it includes the seam allowances. Be sure to mark the pattern name, piece number, and grain-line arrow on the template.

Establishing an Accurate Seam Guide

The most important thing to remember about piecing is to maintain a consistent ¼"-wide seam allowance. Otherwise the quilt block will not finish to the desired size. If the block size is wrong, everything else in the quilt is affected, including alternate blocks, sashings, and borders.

Take the time to establish an exact ¼"-wide seam guide on your machine. Some machines have a special quilting foot designed so that the right and left edges of the foot measure exactly ¼" from the center needle position. This feature allows you to use the edge of the presser foot to guide the edge of the fabric for a perfect ¼"-wide seam allowance.

If your machine doesn't have such a foot, you can create a seam guide so it will be easy to stitch an accurate ¼"-wide seam allowance.

1. Place a ruler or piece of graph paper with 4 squares to the inch under your presser foot.
2. Gently lower the needle onto the first ¼" line from the right edge of the ruler or paper. Place several layers of tape or a piece of moleskin (available in drugstores) along the right edge of the ruler or paper, so that it does not interfere with the feed dogs. Test your new guide to make sure your seams are ¼" wide; if they are not, readjust your guide.

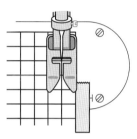

Chain Piecing

Chain piecing is an efficient system that saves time and thread.

1. Begin your chain piecing with a scrap of fabric, called a fabric bridge. Fold a scrap, about 2" to 3" wide, in half, and send it through the machine first.
2. Place the pieces to be joined right sides together. Sew the first pair of pieces, stitching from cut edge to cut edge, using 12 to 15 stitches per inch. At the end of the seam, stop sewing, but do not cut the thread.
3. Feed the next pair of pieces under the presser foot, as close as possible to the first pair.
4. Continue sewing pieces together without cutting the threads between pairs.
5. Before removing the chain from the sewing machine, send another fabric bridge through. Clip the thread between the chain and the fabric bridge. Leave the fabric bridge on the machine to begin the next chain.
6. Clip the threads between the pairs and press the seams.

Be consistent when you chain piece. Start with the same edge on each pair and the same color on top to avoid confusion. There is no need to backstitch, since each seam will be crossed and held by another seam as the assembly process continues.

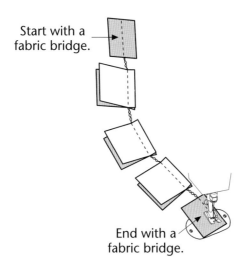

Start with a fabric bridge.

End with a fabric bridge.

Easing

If two pieces being sewn together are slightly different in size (less than ⅛"), pin the places where the two pieces should match, and in the middle if necessary, to distribute the excess fabric evenly. Sew the seam with the longer piece on the bottom. The feed dogs will ease the two pieces together.

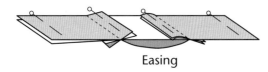

Easing

Bias Squares

One of the easiest and most accurate methods for making bias squares is to cut squares from presewn bias strip units. The squares are accurate because the sewing and pressing are done before the squares are cut. The following method was developed by Mary Hickey. You will need a Bias Square® ruler to cut the required units.

I. Layer the two fabrics to be used for the bias squares, right sides facing up.

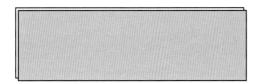

2. Use a ruler with a 45°-angle line to establish a true bias line on the top fabric. Cut bias strips parallel to the drawn line. (Directions for each quilt plan requiring bias squares indicate how many strips to cut and how wide to cut them.)

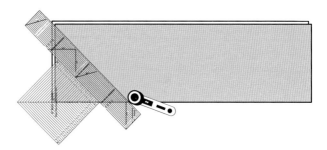

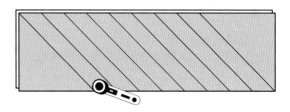

3. Sew the strips together along the bias edges, offsetting the tops of the strips ¼" before stitching as shown. Sew the strips, alternating the fabrics, into units made of 8 to 10 strips. Press seams toward the darker fabrics. When making 1½" or smaller bias squares, press seams open to distribute the bulk.

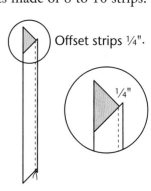

Offset strips ¼".

¼"

4. Position the Bias Square ruler with the diagonal line on a seam line. Place a long ruler across the top to cut an even edge. The trimmed edge should be at a 45° angle to the seam lines.

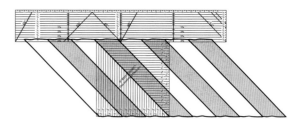

5. Cut a segment parallel to the first cut, cutting the strip the width specified in the quilt plan. Continue cutting segments into the specified widths, making sure to check and correct the angle at the edge after each cut.

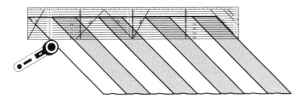

6. Place the Bias Square with the diagonal line on the seam line and one edge of the square on the cut edge of the strip. Cut one side as shown. Continue cutting squares across the remainder of the strip in the same manner.

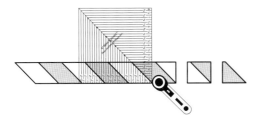

7. Rotate the cut pieces 180°; place the diagonal line of the Bias Square on the seam line and the bottom edge of the ruler on the cut edge of the strip and trim the other edge. To cut squares of the required size, line up the edges of the square with the required markings on the ruler.

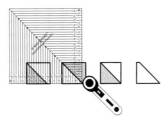

Appliqué Techniques

Usually an appliqué artist has a preferred appliqué technique. My personal favorite is needleturn appliqué. Little preparation time is needed, and with practice the results are pleasing.

If you are just beginning to appliqué, you may want to try various techniques to find one that is comfortable. A technique that works for one needle artist might be cumbersome for another. Refer to *The Easy Art of Appliqué* by Mimi Dietrich and Roxi Eppler for information on appliqué techniques.

Use a long, fine appliqué needle. These needles are called Sharps. The larger the number, the finer the needle. Match the thread as closely as possible to the appliqué fabric, not to the background fabric. Your appliqué stitches will probably not show, but just in case, a matching thread color helps to camouflage any stray stitches.

Baste or pin the appliqué pieces to the background fabric. Small, ½"- to ¾"-long sequin pins work well because they do not get in the way of the thread as you stitch. If you have trouble with threads tangling around pins as you sew, try placing the pins on the underside of your work.

Marking and Cutting Fabric

Make plastic or cardboard templates. Place the template right-side up on the right side of the appliqué fabric. Trace around the shape with a pencil, leaving at least ½" between tracings if several pieces are needed. Cut out each fabric piece, adding ¼"-wide seam allowances around each tracing. This seam allowance will be turned under to create the finished edge of the appliqué. On small pieces, you may wish to add only ⅛", or a scant ¼", for easier handling.

The background fabric is usually a rectangle or square. Cut fabric the required size and shape as given with each project. It is better to cut the background at least one inch larger in each direction to start, then trim it to the correct size after the appliqué has been sewn in place.

Mark the design on the fabric. Place the fabric right-side up over the pattern so that the design is centered. Use a pencil to lightly trace the design. If your background fabric is dark, use a light box, or try taping the pattern to a window or storm door on a sunny day.

Traditional Appliqué Stitch

The traditional appliqué stitch or blind stitch is appropriate for sewing all appliqué shapes, including sharp points and curves.

1. Tie a knot in a single strand of thread, approximately 18" long.

2. Hide the knot by slipping the needle into the seam allowance from the wrong side of the appliqué piece, bringing it out on the fold line.

3. Work from right to left if you are right-handed, or left to right if you are left-handed.

4. Start the first stitch by moving the needle straight off the appliqué, inserting it into the background fabric. Let the needle travel under the background fabric, parallel to the edge of the appliqué, bringing it up about ⅛" away, along the pattern line.

5. As you bring the needle up, pierce the edge of the appliqué piece, catching only 1 or 2 threads of the folded edge.

6. Move the needle straight off the appliqué into the background fabric. Let your needle travel under the background, bringing it up about ⅛" away, again catching the edge of the appliqué.

7. Give the thread a slight tug and continue stitching.

Appliqué stitch

8. To end your stitching, pull the needle through to the wrong side. Behind the appliqué piece, take 2 small stitches, making knots by taking your needle through the loops. Check the right side to see if the thread will "shadow" through your background when finished. If it does, take 1 more small stitch through the back side to direct the tail of the thread under the appliqué fabric.

Stitching Outside Points

As you stitch toward an outside point, start making your stitches closer together within ½" of the point. Trim the seam allowance or push the excess fabric under the point with the tip of your needle. Smaller stitches near the point will keep any frayed edges from escaping.

Place the last stitch on the first side very close to the point. Place the next stitch on the other side of the point. A stitch on each side, close to the point, accents the outside point.

Stitching Along a Curve

Push the fabric under with the tip of your needle, smoothing it out along the folded edge before sewing.

Stitching Inside Points

Make your stitches smaller as you sew within ½" of the point. Stitch past the point, then return to the point to add one extra stitch to emphasize the point. Come up through the appliqué, catching a little more fabric in the inside point (four or five threads instead of one or two). Make a straight stitch outward, going under the point to pull it in a little and emphasize the shape of the point.

If your inside point frays, use a few close stitches to tack the fabric down securely. If your thread matches your appliqué fabric, these stitches will blend in with the edge of the shape.

Needleturn Appliqué

I prefer this method because you do not turn under and baste the seam allowances in preparation for appliquéing.

1. Using a plastic template, trace the design onto the right side of the appliqué fabric.
2. Cut out the fabric piece, adding a *scant* ¼"-wide seam allowance.
3. Position the appliqué piece on the background fabric and pin or baste in place.
4. Starting on a straight edge, use the tip of the needle to gently turn under the seam allowance, about ½" at a time. Hold the turned seam allowance firmly between the thumb and first finger of your left hand (reverse if left-handed) as you stitch the appliqué to the background. Use a longer needle, a Sharp or milliner's needle, to help you control the seam allowance and turn it under neatly.

Cut-As-You-Go Appliqué

This is also a needleturn method of appliqué; however, the design is cut from the fabric as you stitch, not before. This method is recommended for large appliqué pieces.

1. Using a plastic template, trace the design onto the right side of the appliqué fabric. The fabric should be just a bit larger than the design you are tracing. Do not cut out the design yet.
2. Pin or baste the appliqué fabric in place on the background fabric.
3. Cut away the fabric 2" to 3" ahead of your stitching, leaving a ⅛" to ¼"-wide seam allowance beyond the traced line. Use the needleturn method described above to appliqué the design, cutting and turning the fabric as you go. Turn the fabric under so that the traced line is not visible.

Perfect Circles

To take the headache out of trying to make perfect circles, I use adhesive dots, found at office supply stores. The dots come in several sizes. To use them, place the sticky side on the wrong side of the fabric and finger-press the fabric over the edges of the circle.

Pin or baste the circle in place and appliqué around the edges. Before finishing the last few stitches on the circle, peel the dot from behind the fabric; then finish appliquéing the circle.

Adding Borders

For best results, do not cut border strips and sew them directly to the quilt sides without measuring first. This method often results in a quilt with wavy borders. The edges of a quilt often measure slightly longer than the distance through the quilt center, due to stretching during construction. Measure the quilt top through the center in both directions to determine how long to cut the border strips. This step ensures that the finished quilt will be as straight and as "square" as possible, without wavy edges.

Plain border strips are commonly cut along the crosswise grain and seamed when extra length is needed. Borders cut from the lengthwise grain of the fabric require extra yardage, but seaming the required length is not necessary.

You can add borders that have straight-cut or mitered corners.

Straight-Cut Borders

1. Measure the length of the quilt top through the center. Cut border strips to that measurement, piecing as necessary. Mark the centers of the quilt top and the border strips. Pin the borders to the sides of the quilt top, matching the center marks and ends, and easing as necessary. Sew the border strips in place. Press the seams toward the border.

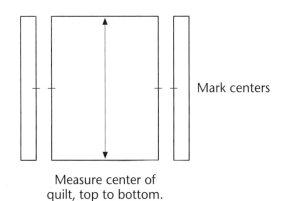

Mark centers

Measure center of
quilt, top to bottom.

2. Measure the width of the quilt through the center, including the side borders just added. Cut border strips to that measurement, piecing as necessary. Mark the center of the quilt top and the border strips. Pin the borders to the sides of the quilt top, matching the center marks and ends and easing as necessary. Sew the border strips in place. Press seams toward the border.

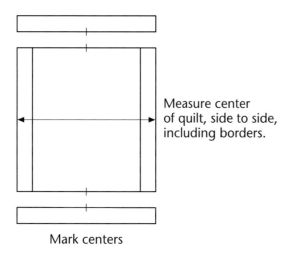

Measure center of quilt, side to side, including borders.

Mark centers

Borders with Mitered Corners

I. First estimate the finished outside dimensions of your quilt, including borders. Cut border strips to this length, plus at least ½" for seam allowances. It's safer to add 2" to 3" to give yourself some leeway. Cut border strips, piecing as necessary, to match these lengths.

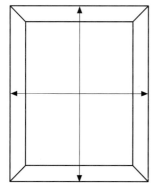

Estimate outside dimensions, including borders.

NOTE: If your quilt has multiple borders, sew the individual strips together and treat the resulting unit as a single border strip. This makes mitering corners easier and more accurate.

2. Measure the length and width of the quilt across the center. Note the measurements.

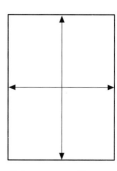

Measure quilt top without borders.

3. Fold the quilt in half and mark the centers of the quilt edges. Fold each border strip in half and mark each center with a pin.

4. Place a pin at each end of the side border strips to mark the length of the quilt top. Repeat with the top and bottom borders.

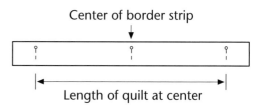

Center of border strip

Length of quilt at center

5. Matching the centers and pins on the border strip to the ends of the quilt top, stitch the borders to the quilt with a ¼"-wide seam. The border strip should extend the same distance at each end of the quilt. Start and stop your stitching ¼" from the corners of the quilt. Press the seams toward the borders.

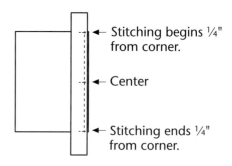

Stitching begins ¼" from corner.

Center

Stitching ends ¼" from corner.

6. Lay the first corner to be mitered on the ironing board. Fold one strip under at a 45° angle and adjust so seam lines match perfectly. Press and pin.

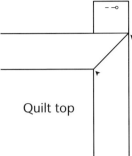

Quilt top

7. Fold the quilt with right sides together, lining up the edges of the border. If necessary, use a ruler to draw a pencil line on the crease to make the line more visible. Stitch on the pressed crease, sewing from corner to outside edge.

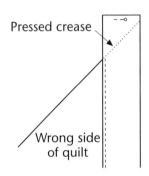

Pressed crease

Wrong side of quilt

NOTE: If the quilt is large, sometimes it is easier to sew the 45° angle on the border with a blind stitch. This avoids maneuvering a large quilt through the sewing machine and distorting the angle.

8. Press the seam open and trim away excess border strips, leaving a ¼"-wide seam allowance.
9. Repeat with the remaining corners.

Finishing Techniques

This section includes techniques you need to use to finish the quilts in this book.

Marking Quilting Lines

Whether or not to mark quilting designs depends upon the type of quilting you will be doing. Marking is not necessary if you plan to quilt in-the-ditch, or outline quilt a uniform distance from seam lines. Mark complex quilting designs on the quilt top *before* the quilt is layered with batting and backing.

Choose a marking tool that will be visible on your fabric, and test it on fabric scraps to be sure you can easily remove the marks. Masking tape can also be used to mark straight quilting. Tape only small sections at a time, and remove the tape when you stop at the end of the day; otherwise, it may be difficult to remove the sticky residue from the fabric.

Care of the Quilter

Consider your eyes when quilting and doing handwork. Work with plenty of natural or artificial light on your project. A direct light source on your appliqué or quilting avoids eye strain and makes it easier to see where you are going. If you wear glasses, tell your eye doctor that you are a quilter. Show the doctor the distance that you hold your detailed work from your eyes. This will ensure an understanding of your vision requirements.

Layering the Quilt

Backing

Use 100% cotton fabric for the backing. You can use a beautiful print for the backing or piece the left-overs from the quilt front to make a backing.

Cut the backing so that it extends 2" to 4" beyond the outer edges of the quilt top. For large quilts, piece two or three lengths of fabric together to make a backing of the required size. Press the backing seams open to make quilting easier.

 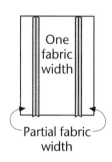

One fabric width

Two lengths of fabric seamed in the center

Partial fabric width

NOTE: The back of a quilt often offers as much visual excitement as the front. Wholecloth backs are often beautiful pieces of fabric. If early quiltmakers did not have the means or the opportunity to obtain a large fabric piece, they often pieced together strips or squares from a scrapbag. These fabrics offer many clues in the dating of a quilt.

Batting

Choose a batting based on the appearance you desire for your quilt and the quilting method you intend to use. Thick battings are fine for tied quilts and comforters; a thinner batting is better, however, if you intend to quilt by hand or machine. All-cotton batting is soft and drapeable but requires close quilting, while polyester and cotton-polyester battings require less quilting. The intended use of the quilt may also dictate which batting you should choose. Your local quilt shop staff will be able to help you choose the right batting.

Whatever the batting choice, plan ahead and un-wrap the batting a day or two before it is needed to allow it to relax and expand before being layered in your quilt. Cut the batting so that it extends 2" to 4" beyond the outer edges of the quilt top.

To layer the quilt:

1. Spread the backing, wrong side up, on a flat, clean surface. Anchor it with pins or masking tape. Be careful not to stretch the backing out of shape.
2. Spread the batting over the backing, smoothing out any wrinkles.
3. Place the pressed quilt top on top of the batting. Smooth out any wrinkles and make sure the edges of the quilt top are parallel to the edges of the backing.
4. Baste with needle and thread, starting in the center and working diagonally to each corner. Continue basting, in a grid of horizontal and vertical lines 6" to 8" apart. Finish by basting around the edges.

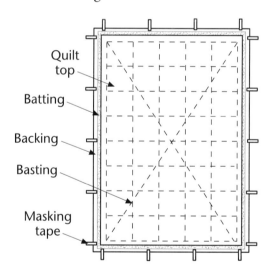

Quilt top

Batting

Backing

Basting

Masking tape

NOTE: Baste the layers with #2 rust-proof safety pins for machine quilting. Place pins about 6" to 8" apart, away from the area you intend to quilt.

5. Turn the back over the raw edges of the quilt front and baste; this prevents the quilt from becoming worn before the binding is applied.

Quilting

Quilting stitches play two important roles in a quilt. On the practical side, they hold the three layers of the quilt together (the quilt top, batting, and backing). On the artistic side, they add detail and depth to the quilt.

To quilt by hand, you need short, sturdy needles (called Betweens), quilting thread, and a thimble to fit the middle finger of your sewing hand. Most quilters also use a frame or hoop to support their work. Quilting needles run from size 3 to 12; the higher the number, the smaller the needle. Use the smallest needle you can comfortably handle; the smaller the needle, the smaller your stitches will be.

1. Thread your needle with a single strand of quilting thread about 18" long; make a small knot and insert the needle in the top layer about 1" from the place you want to start stitching. Pull the needle out at the point where quilting will begin and gently pull the thread until the knot pops through the fabric and into the batting.

2. Take small, evenly spaced stitches through all 3 quilt layers.

3. Rock the needle up and down through all layers, until you have 3 or 4 stitches on the needle. Place your other hand underneath the quilt so you can feel the needle point with the tip of your finger when a stitch is taken.

4. To end a line of quilting, make a small knot close to the last stitch; then backstitch, running the thread a needle's length through the batting. Gently pull the thread until the knot pops into the batting. Clip the thread at the quilt's surface.

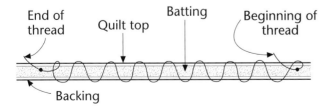

For more information on hand quilting, refer to *Loving Stitches* by Jeanna Kimball.

Binding the Edges

Adding the binding is one of the last steps in making your quilt, but it is one of the most important for the quilt's appearance. Make bindings from straight-grain or bias strips of fabric. I use a straight-grain, double-fold binding for a durable finish with a neat appearance. Use bias binding strips for quilts with curved edges.

NOTE: If you want to attach a sleeve or rod pocket to the back of the quilt, see page 83 for making the sleeve prior to attaching the binding.

To cut straight-grain binding strips:
Cut 2¼"-wide strips across the width of the fabric. You will need enough strips to go around the perimeter of the quilt plus 10" for seams and the corners in a mitered fold.

To cut bias binding strips:
1. Fold a square of fabric on the diagonal;

Or, fold a ½-yard piece as shown below, paying careful attention to the location of the lettered corners.

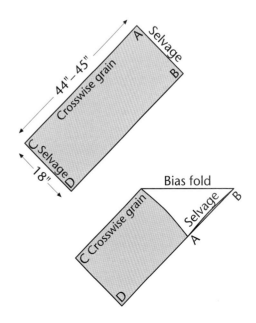

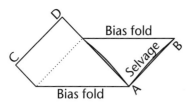

2. Cut strips 2¼" wide, cutting perpendicular to the folds as shown.

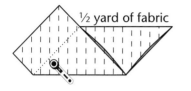

To attach binding:

1. Trim the batting and backing even with the quilt top edges.
2. Sew binding strips together to make one long piece of binding. Press the seams open.

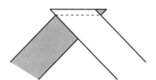 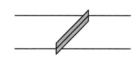

If you cut strips on the straight grain, join strips at right angles and stitch across the corner as shown. Trim excess fabric and press seams open.

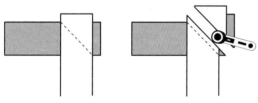

Joining Straight-Cut Strips

3. Turn under ¼" at a 45° angle at one end of the strip and press. Turning the end under at an angle distributes the bulk so you won't have a lump where the two ends of the binding meet. Fold the strip in half lengthwise, wrong sides together, and press.

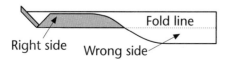

4. Starting on one side of the quilt, stitch the binding to the quilt, keeping the raw edges even with the quilt top edge. Use a ¼"-wide seam allowance. End the stitching ¼" from the corner of the quilt and backstitch. Clip the thread.

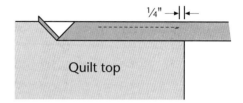

5. Turn the quilt so that you will be stitching down the next side. Fold the binding up, away from the quilt.

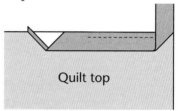

6. Fold the binding back down onto itself, parallel with the edge of the quilt top. Begin stitching at the edge, backstitching to secure.

7. Repeat on the remaining edges and corners of the quilt. When you reach the beginning of the binding, overlap the beginning stitches by about 1" and cut away any excess binding, trimming the end at a 45° angle. Tuck the end of the binding into fold and finish the seam.

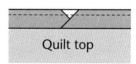

8. Fold the binding over the raw edges of the quilt to the back and blindstitch in place with the folded edge covering the row of machine stitching. A miter will form at each corner. Blindstitch the mitered corners in place.

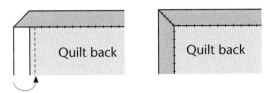

Hanging Sleeves

If you plan to display your finished quilts on the wall, be sure to add a hanging sleeve to hold the rod.

I. Using leftover fabric from the front or a piece of muslin, cut a strip 8½" wide and 1" shorter than the width of the quilt at the top edge. Fold the ends under ½", then under ½" again, and stitch.

½" ½"

2. Fold the fabric strip in half lengthwise, *wrong sides together,* and baste the raw edges to the top edge of the back of your quilt. The top edge of the sleeve will be secured when the binding is sewn to the quilt.

3. Push the bottom edge of the sleeve up just a bit to provide a little give so the hanging rod does not put strain on the quilt itself. Blindstitch the bottom of the sleeve in place.

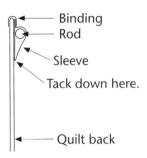

Quilt Labels

A label for your quilt is so very important! Please let the world know that you made the quilt. Someday, a great-grandchild napping under your quilt will read your name and feel a special closeness to you. Include the following information on your label:

★ Maker's name
★ Quilter's name
★ Town and state where quilt was made
★ Year made
★ Information unique to the quilt

Before stitching the label to the quilt, consider writing your name and address in permanent ink on the back of the quilt where the label will be attached. If the label were ever removed, the name would still be there.

Also, consider sewing the label to the quilt before quilting. Quilt through the label. This is the most permanent label and will never be removed.

Resources

For the hand-dyed fabric in "Hexagonal Magic" and "Crossed Laurel Leaves," contact:

Country House Cottons
Milly and Kim Churbuck
Box 375
Fayette, IA 52142
(319) 425–4384

Memberships available:
American Quilt Study Group
660 Mission Street, Suite 400
San Francisco, CA 94105-4007

Bibliography

Brackman, Barbara. *An Encyclopedia of Pieced Quilt Patterns.* Lawrence, Kan.: Prairie Flower Publishing, 1984.

Clark, Ricky. *Quilted Gardens, Floral Quilts of the Nineteenth Century.* Nashville, Tenn.: Rutledge Hill Press, 1994.

Hall, Carrie A. and Rose G. Kretsinger. *The Romance of the Patchwork Quilt in America.* New York: Bonanza Books, 1935.

Khin, Yvonne M. *The Collector's Dictionary of Quilt Names & Patterns.* Washington, D. C.: Acropolis Books Ltd., 1980.

McKim, Ruby Short. *101 Patchwork Patterns.* New York: Dover Publications, Inc., 1962.

Miles, Elaine. *Quilts and Quotes, A Birthday Book.* San Pedro, Calif.: R. & E. Miles, 1981.

Rehmel, Judy. *The Quilt I. D. Book.* New York: Prentice Hall Press, 1986.

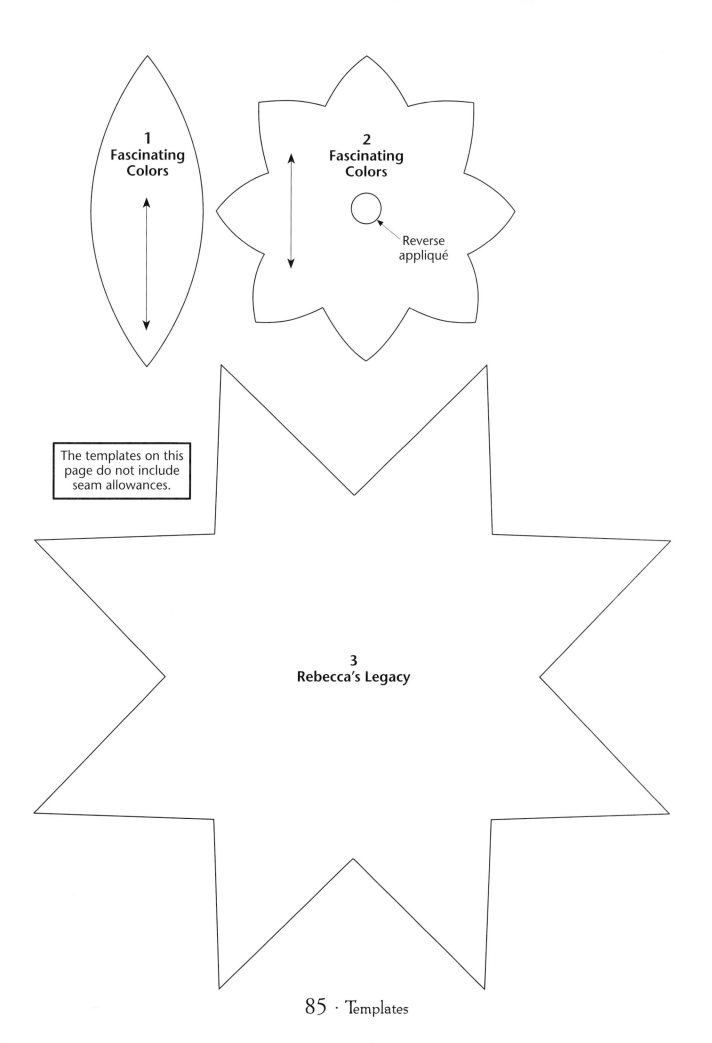

1
Fascinating Colors

2
Fascinating Colors

Reverse appliqué

The templates on this page do not include seam allowances.

3
Rebecca's Legacy

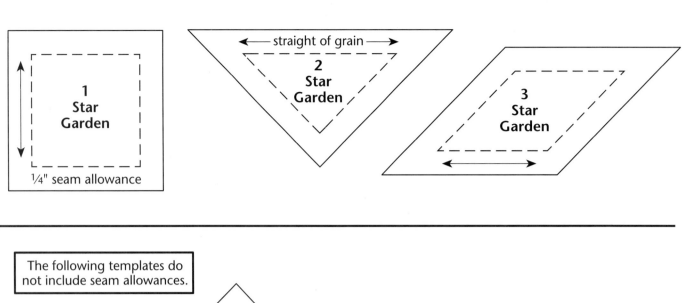

1
Star
Garden

¼" seam allowance

straight of grain

2
Star
Garden

3
Star
Garden

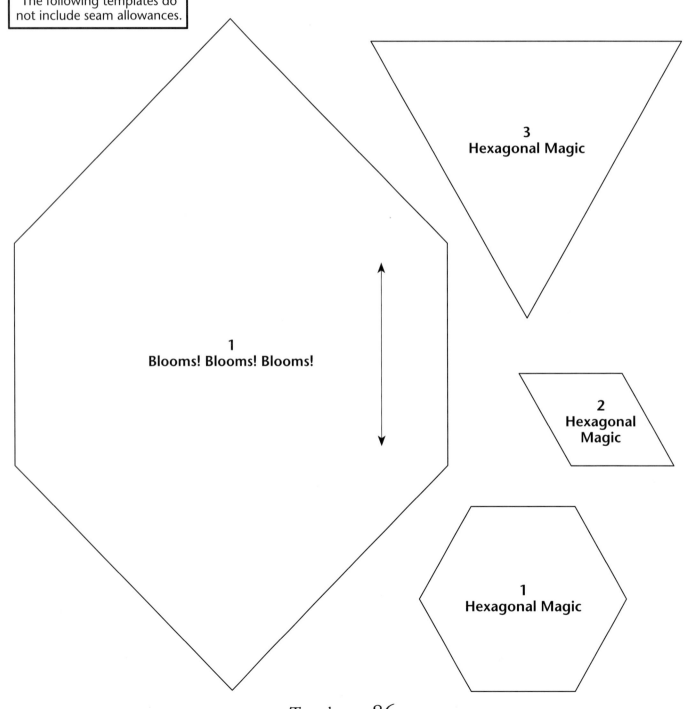

The following templates do not include seam allowances.

1
Blooms! Blooms! Blooms!

3
Hexagonal Magic

2
Hexagonal
Magic

1
Hexagonal Magic

About the Author

Sara Rhodes Dillow learned to quilt in 1980. She enjoys every facet of quilting and strives to experience all that it offers. Her favorite technique is whatever she is using on her current project.

The first president of the Nebraska State Quilt Guild, Sara is currently the chair of NSQG's pioneering Quilt Preservation Project, an endeavor to document and provide quilt preservation and storage enhancements for museum quilt collections throughout Nebraska. Sara was recently elected to the Nebraska State Quilt Guild's Hall of Fame. As a new board member of the American Quilt Study Group,

Sara believes in preserving the stories behind quilts and encouraging quilt history researchers.

Sara has combined a love of quilts and nature by creating a series of notecards that show quilts photographed in natural settings. These photographs have been featured in *Nebraska-land* and *Quilter's Newsletter Magazine*.

Sara and her husband, Byron, have three grown children. The family welcomed the first member of the next generation with the arrival of Megan in November 1994. In addition to family and quilting, Sara enjoys gardening, antique collecting, bird watching, and photography.

That Patchwork Place Publications and Products